AQA GCSE ANTHOLOGY:

LOVE AND RELATIONSHIPS –

THE STUDENT GUIDE

DAVID WHEELER

Red Axe Books

ISBN: 978-0993218354

Find as at:

www.dogstailbooks.co.uk

The painting on the cover is 'Primavera' (Spring) by Botticelli.

CONTENTS

Introduction

I hope you find this revision guide useful. It consists of an individual analysis of each poem in the AQA Anthology – Love and Relationships. The analysis of each poem follows the same pattern: there is a section on the poet and the context in which the poem was written and some facts about each author; unfamiliar words are explained; and then each poem has a commentary which focuses on both what the poem is about and the style, form and structure that the poet uses. A final section on each poem summarizes the poem's overall impact and effect. There are no colours, few illustrations, but you will get a clear sense of what each poem is about and each poem's overall effect.

Who or what is this book for?

Perhaps you missed that crucial lesson on one particular poem that you find hard to understand? Good lessons are better than this book, because through different activities and through careful questioning and probing your teacher will help you to arrive at an understanding, an appreciation of the poem that you work out for yourself – and that process is invaluable – it's a process of thinking and exploring as a group, in a pair perhaps and as an individual, and, no matter how good the notes that your class-mates made, those notes are no substitute for having been there and gone through the process of the lesson. So, maybe, through absence, you feel a little out of touch with some of the poems: this book will help you.

Alternatively you may want to read about ideas which you have not encountered in class. Alternatively you may have the sort of teacher who allows you to respond in your own way to the poems; that is a completely valid and worthwhile approach, of course, but it does not suit every student: some students like to have clear guidelines about the meaning of what they read and to have various interpretations suggested to them so that they are at least aware of the overall gist of the poem. It still leaves you free to make up your own mind and have your own ideas, but it does provide a starting point – this book will give you that starting point.

You may be trying to revise the poems in the final days and weeks before the exam and want a quick refresher on poems that you first studied in class a long time ago; maybe it was a Friday afternoon and you weren't paying complete attention; maybe you were late for the lesson and never quite 'got' what the poem is about; maybe you were distracted by something more interesting happening outside and spent the lesson gazing out of the window. This book will help you get to grips with that those poems.

It is very unlikely, but you may be reading these poems on your own for the very first time – this book will help you too, because I have assumed that you know nothing about the poem or about poetry, and the commentary on each poem is written so that you can start from scratch. Of course, some of you might find this a tiny bit condescending – and I apologize for that. I should also apologize if there are ideas in this book which are different from ones you have encountered before in class. There are as many different ways to read a poem as there are readers, and each reader might have a slightly different view of a particular poem – as we shall see. For example, most readers (pupils, teachers, professional critics) would agree that 'London' by William Blake is critical of the society he lives in; most would agree that 'London' is a bitter attack on the London that he lived in, but quite what the final verse means is open to a variety of interpretations!

So... if you want a book that tells you what each poem means; comments on features of style and structure; suggests the tone or the overall impact of each poem; gives you the necessary background knowledge to understand each poem – then this is it. At the end you will find a glossary of poetic terms, but after this introduction, there is a commentary on each poem – each commentary is self-contained and can be read on its own. Throughout the book I have used the words that I would use if I were teaching a lesson on these poems – if I use words you don't know or haven't heard, then look them up. Part of education, part of writing well about Literature is the way you yourself write, so to expand your vocabulary is a good thing. Terms which have specific literary meanings are all in the glossary at the back of the book.

Help Yourself!

I hope you find this book helpful in some ways, perhaps many ways. It deliberately does not include very detailed information about the authors for two reasons. Firstly, it would be a waste of space. Secondly, the internet is a rich source of information about writers and their work – an internet search on any of your studied poets or poems will throw up all sorts of interesting resources, including student chat boards, online revision chat-rooms as well as more obvious sources of information like Wikipedia or web sites associated with a particular author. Where there is detailed biographical information here, it is because it is vital to an understanding of the poem.

But do be warned – all the information you can possibly find about a particular poet may help to clarify something you already sensed about the poem, but it is no substitute for engagement with the poem itself. And in the examination the examiner does <u>not</u> want to read a potted biography of the poet whose poem you have chosen to write about. Besides - generalizing from what we know about a writer or his/her era is a dangerous thing: for example, it is important to be aware of William Blake's political beliefs and to be aware that he wrote 'London' during the years of the French Revolution – some might say that without such an awareness the poem cannot be fully appreciated and understood – BUT that will not help you explain the impact of individual words and lines and images at all, nor will it help you write well in the examination. Very often I have started my commentary on a poem with necessary information to help you understand it, but you don't need to reproduce all that information in the exam - it is there to help you fully understand significant details about the poem; to try to reproduce the process of discovery that a good lesson will guide you through. But it probably has little place in the examination.

You may be the sort of student who is doing English Language or English Literature because it is compulsory at your school. But it may also be that as you progress through the course you come to feel that English is a subject that you like and are good at; you may even be intrigued or fascinated by some of the poems in the anthology. If that happens, then do not rely on this book. Look on the internet for resources that will further your interest. For example, if one poet makes a special impact on you – read some of their other work; you will find a lot of it available on-line. Many of the poets in the Literary Heritage sections are now out of copyright – their work is freely available on-line. Many of the contemporary poets have their own websites which can be a fascinating source of extra information and contain links to other poems or biographical information. So there are many ways in which you can help yourself: it's a good habit to get into, especially if you start thinking about the possibility of doing English at A level.

But please remember this is no substitute for a close engagement with the poems themselves. And just as importantly – this book is no substitute for a good lesson which allows you to think about the poem's language and ideas, and then slowly come to an understanding of it. After understanding it (and that is an emotional as much as a logical understanding of it), you may come to appreciate it. What does that mean? Well, as you go through the course and read more and more poems then you may find that you prefer some to others. The next step is to identify why you prefer some poems to others: in this there are no right answers, but there are answers which are clearer and better expressed than others. And preference must be based on reasons to do with the way the poem is written or its overall emotional impact: it's your job to put what you think and feel into words – I cannot help you do that. I can merely point out some of the important features and meanings of the poems. As you grow in confidence and perhaps read other writing on these poems or listening to your teacher or your classmates, then you will start to formulate your own opinions – stealing an idea from one person, a thought from somewhere else and combining all these different things into your own view of the poem. And that is appreciation. As soon as you say you prefer one poem to another you are engaging in a critical reaction to what you have read – in exactly the same way that people prefer one film to another or one song or performer to another.

Romanticism

In this cluster of poems the first three are designated Romantic poems and it is important that you have an understanding of what Romanticism was. It has very little to do with the word 'romantic' as we apply it today to an event like Valentine's Day.

Romanticism is the name given to the artistic, political and cultural movement that emerged in England and Germany in the 1790s and in the rest of Europe in the 1820s and beyond. It was a movement that saw great changes in literature, painting, sculpture, architecture and music, and found its catalyst in the new philosophical ideas of Jean Jacques Rousseau and Thomas Paine, and in response to the American, French and industrial revolutions. Its chief emphasis was on freedom of individual self-expression, sincerity, spontaneity and originality, but it also looked to the distant past of the Middle Ages for some of its inspiration. In Romantic thought the nature of the poet changed: no longer was a poet someone who could manipulate words well and with skill; the poet was a special individual with a unique vision to communicate and with special insights to communicate through his poetry.

The key characteristics of Romantic poetry in English are:

- a reverence for and veneration of the natural world.
- a belief that the poet was a special person who had important truths to communicate and whose experiences were more intense than those of ordinary people.
- an emphasis on individualism and intense emotion.

- a increased interest in ordinary people – the rural poor and the urban working classes.
- a political radicalism, best summed up by the watchwords of the French Revolution – liberty, fraternity, equality.
- an overwhelming emphasis on the sensibility and imagination of the poet.
- an interest in medieval and ancient history.
- a veneration of Shakespeare.
- a desire to be original and to reject the orthodoxies of the immediate past.

Of course, not all the poets that we label 'Romantic' displayed all these characteristics all through their careers.

Contemporary Poetry & the Literary Heritage

You will probably have noticed that the poems within each section or cluster of your anthology are designated as Literary Heritage poems. Why? Contemporary poetry consists of poems written in the very recent past by living poets and they are here because as you study English or English Literature, it is felt to be important that you realize that poetry is not dead and poetry is not only written by dead white Englishmen: it is alive and it is being written now all over the English-speaking world by men and by women from a wide variety of backgrounds. So the contemporary poems are there to remind you that poetry is alive and well and thriving. Indeed, as I have already mentioned, many of the contemporary poets have their own websites or perform poetry readings which you may be lucky enough to attend during your course. You can also see some performances of these poems on the internet.

The poems in the first half of the anthology are generally by dead white Englishmen, although there are some poems by women. That sounds dismissive (dead white Englishmen), but it's not meant to be. They are in the anthology to remind you that writers have been writing poetry in English for hundreds of years and that what happens over those centuries is that an agreement emerges about which poems are some of the greatest or most significant ever written in the English Language. How does such agreement emerge? Well, mainly through people continuing to read the poems, responding to them and enjoying them; another concrete way is for the poems to appear in anthologies – which ensures them an even wider audience. The point you need to grasp is that writing in English poetry has been going on for hundreds of years and what has been written in the past influences what is written now. Many contemporary poets will have read the poems that you will read in the Literary Heritage sections. So when you read, for example, 'Love's Philosophy' by Percy Shelley for the first time, you will be joining the millions of English-speaking people all over the world who have read and enjoyed that sonnet. Organizations like the BBC have also run public votes where members of the public can vote for their favourite poem – another way that we know which poems are popular. Such poems then become part of the canon' such as those by Robert Browning and his wife, Elizabeth Barrett Browning That is not to say, however, that there is only agreement about the value of poems from the distant past: some like those by Charles Causley and Seamus Heaney are from the closing decades of the 20th century; they are included because already there is widespread agreement that these poets are important and influential and that their poems are rewarding to read and study and enjoy.

So part of our heritage, part of the culture of speaking English, whether you speak English in Delhi or London or Manchester or Lahore or Trinidad or Liverpool or Auckland or Toronto or Cape Town or Chicago, is centuries of English poetry and a continuing poetic culture which is rich and vibrant, and includes voices from all over the English-speaking world.

The Secret of Poetry

The secret of poetry, of course, is that there is no secret. Nonetheless, I have come across lots of students who find poetry challenging or off-putting or who don't like it for some reason. I find this attitude bizarre for all sorts of reasons. But some students are very wary of poetry or turned off by it. If you are – rest assured: you shouldn't be!

Poetry is all around us: in proverbial sayings, in popular music, in the nursery rhymes we listen to or sing as children, in playground skipping chants, even in the chanting heard at football matches. All these things use the basic elements of poetry: rhythm and rhyming and very often the techniques of poetry – alliteration, repetition, word play. Advertisements and newspaper headlines also use these techniques to make what they say memorable. Ordinary everyday speech is full of poetry: if you say that something is 'as cheap as chips' you are using alliteration and a simile; if you think someone is 'two sandwiches short of a picnic', if someone is 'a pain in the arse', then you are using metaphors – the only difference is that when poets use similes and metaphors they try to use ones that are fresh and original – and memorable, in the same away that a nursery rhyme or your favourite song lyrics are memorable. Even brand names or shop names use some of the techniques of poetry: if you have a Kwik Fit exhaust supplier in your town you should note the word-play (the mis-spelling of Kwik) and the assonance – the repetition of the 'i' sound. There must be several hundred ladies' hairdressers in the UK called 'Curl Up and Dye' -- which is comic word-play. You may go to 'Fat Face' because you like what they sell, but I hope that when you go next time, you'll spare a thought for the alliteration and assonance in the shop's name.

Poets also play with words. So when students tell me they don't like poetry, I don't believe them – I feel they have simply not approached it in the right way. Or perhaps not seen the link between the poetry of everyday life and the poetry they have to study and analyze for GCSE.

Poetry has been around a very long time: the earliest surviving literature in Europe consists of poetry. As far as we can tell poetry existed even before writing, and so poems were passed down by word of mouth for centuries before anyone bothered to write them down. If something is going to be passed down and remembered in this way, then it has to be memorable. And, as we shall see, poets use various techniques and tricks and patterns to make what they write easy to remember or striking in some way - just as you may remember the words to your favourite song or to a nursery rhyme that was recited to you as a small child. Let us take one example. The opening sentence of Charles Dickens' novel *A Tale of Two Cities* is

It was the best of times; it was the worst of times.

It is not poetry, but it is very memorable, because Dickens uses simple repetition, parallelism and paradox to create a very memorable sentence. Parallelism because the two halves of the sentence are the same – except for one word; and paradox because the two words – best and worst – seem to contradict each other. Now look at this recent slogan from an advert for Jaguar cars:

Don't dream it. Drive it.

This uses the same techniques as Dickens: parallelism and paradox (or juxtaposition) and it also uses alliteration. It is all about manipulating words to give them greater impact – to make them memorable.

As I am sure I will repeat elsewhere, it is always vital to read a poem aloud: your teacher might do it very well, you might be lucky enough to hear one of the living poets in the anthology read their poems aloud or you can access many recordings via the internet. I think reading a poem aloud is a good way to revise it: it has been claimed that when we read something aloud we are reading twenty times slower than when we read with our eyes – and that slowness is vital, because it allows the sound of the poem, the turn of each phrase and the rhythm of each poem to stand out. As we shall see, the way a poem sounds is absolutely crucial to its impact – for one thing, it helps you pick out techniques such as alliteration and assonance.

One of the things we will discover is that poetry is partly about pattern – patterns of sounds, of words, of rhythm; patterns of lay-out too, so that a poem and the way it is set out on the page - often separated into separate stanzas (don't call them verses) – is vital. If you quickly glance at a page from the anthology, you would probably assume that what is on the page is a poem – because we have certain expectations of the way that poems look. So what? You have probably been aware for a long time that poets often organize what they write into stanzas. For me this an absolutely crucial part of poetry because as human beings we are in love with patterns, we are addicted to patterns – and that is one of the many reasons we love poetry or find it so appealing. Patterns dominate our lives. We may have patterns on our clothes, our furnishings, our curtains, our carpets. But patterns rule our lives more completely than that: seen from above even a housing estate has patterns – the street lights at regular intervals, the garages and gardens in the same relationship to the houses; a spider's web on a frosty morning; the unique patterns of snowflakes; a honeycomb; your school uniform perhaps; the rhythm of your day, of the timetable you follow at school, of your week, of the seasons and of the year. And where patterns do not exist we like to invent them: the periodic table of elements (which you may be familiar with from Chemistry) does not exist as a table out there in nature – it's the human need to organize and give things a pattern which is responsible for the way it looks. Or look at a map of the world, criss-crossed by lines of longitude and latitude – and invented by the human mind as an aid for navigation.

What on earth has this to do with poetry? Well, poetry, especially from the past, likes to follow patterns and this structure that poets choose is something we instinctively like; it is also important when poets set up a pattern, only to break it to make whatever they are saying even more memorable because it breaks the pattern. We will see this happen in some of the poems in the anthology.

Let us look at it another way. Take the sonnet: if you choose to write a sonnet, you are committing yourself to trying to say what you want to say in 140 syllables, arranged in equal lines of 10 syllables each and fitted to a complex rhyming scheme. It is very hard to do, so why bother?

Partly because it is a challenge – to force you to condense what you want to say into 140 syllables concentrates the mind and, more importantly, makes for language that can be very condensed and full of meaning. And, of course, the sonnet has been around for centuries so to choose to write one now means you are following (and hoping to bring something new and surprising) to a long-established form.

So what is poetry? *The Oxford Concise Dictionary of Literary Terms* defines it as:

Language sung, chanted, spoken, or written according to some pattern of recurrence that emphasizes the relationships between words on the basis of sound as well as sense: this pattern is almost always a rhythm or metre, which may be supplemented by rhyme or alliteration or both. All cultures have their poetry, using it for various purposes from sacred ritual to obscene insult, but it is generally employed in those utterances and writings that call for heightened intensity of emotion, dignity of expression, or subtlety of meditation. Poetry is valued for combining pleasures of sound with freshness of ideas....

Remember some of these phrases as you read this book or as you read the poems in the Anthology – which poems have intensity of emotion? Are there some which have a freshness of ideas? Or do some make you think about things more deeply (subtlety of meditation)? Perhaps there are poems which make you do all three? What can I possibly add to the Oxford Book of Literary Terms? Think of your favourite song – whatever type of music you listen to. The song's lyrics will share many of the characteristics of poetry, but the words will be enhanced by the music and the delivery of the vocalist. Is it a song that makes you happy or sad? Angry or mellow? Whatever it makes you feel, a song takes you on an emotional journey – and that is what poems do too, except they lack musical accompaniment. So think of a poem as being like a song – designed to make you feel a particular emotion and think particular thoughts; like some songs, the emotions, the thoughts, may be quiet complex and hard to explain but the similarity is there. And that is another reason why it is important to hear the poems read aloud – they are designed to be listened to, not simply read. Short poems like the ones in the Anthology are often called lyric poems – and that is because hundreds of years ago they would have been accompanied by music. Before 1066 Anglo-Saxon bards telling even long narrative poems used to accompany themselves on a lyre – a primitive type of guitar and up to Elizabethan times lyric poems were set to music and performed.

Making Connections

As you can see from what is written above, a lot of the work in English on the Anthology is about making connections – the exam question will explicitly ask you to do this. As you study the Anthology or read this book you should try to make connections for yourself. Free your mind and make unusual connections. You might feel that some poems take you on a similar emotional journey; some poems might use metaphor or personification in similar ways; some poems were written at the same time as others and are connected by their context.

If you can connect poems because of their written style or something like structure or technique, then that will impress the examiner more than if you simply connect them by subject matter. The poems are already connected by simply being in the Anthology, so to start an answer, for example, by stating that two poems are about 'Conflict' is a waste of words. You should try to do some thinking for yourself as you read this book and reflect on the poems in the anthology– because it is a good habit to get into and helps prepare you mentally for the exam.

Do you have a favourite word? If you do, you might like to think about why you like it so much. It may well have something to do with the meaning, but it might also have something to do with the sound. Of course, some words are clearly onomatopoeic like *smash*, *bang* and *crack*. But other words have sound qualities too which alter the way we react to them – and they are not obviously onomatopoeic. For example, the word *blister* sounds quite harsh because the letter *b* and the combination of *st* sound a little unpleasant; and, of course, we know what a *blister* is and it is not a pleasant thing. On the other hand, words like *fearful* or *gentle* or *lightly* have a lighter, more delicate sound because of the letters from which they are made. Words like *glitter* and *glisten* cannot be onomatopoeic: onomatopoeia is all about imitating the sound that something makes and *glitter* and *glisten* refer to visual phenomena, but the the *gl* at the start and the *st* and *tt* in the middle of the words make them sound entirely appropriate, just right, don't they?

Think of it another way: just reflect on the number of swear words or derogatory terms in English which start with *b* or *p*: *bloody, bugger, bastard, plonker, pratt, prick, prawn* – the list goes on and on. The hard *c* sound in a word like *cackle* is also unpleasant to the ear. So what? Well, as you read poems try to be aware of this, because poets often choose light, gentle sounds to create a gentle atmosphere: listen to the sounds. Of course, the meaning of the word is the dominant element that we respond to, but listen to it as well.

You don't need to know anything about the history of the English language to get a good grade at GCSE. However, where our language comes from makes English unique. English was not spoken in the British Isles until about 450 CE when tribes from what is now Holland invaded as the Roman Empire gradually collapsed. The language these tribes spoke is now known as Old English – if you were to see some it would look very foreign to your eyes, but it is where our basic vocabulary comes from. A survey once picked out the hundred words that are most used in written English: ninety-nine of them had their roots in Old English; the other one was derived from French. The French the Normans spoke had developed from Latin and so when we look at English vocabulary – all the words that are in the dictionary – we can make a simple distinction between words that come from Old English and words that come from Latin – either directly from Latin or from Latin through French. [I am ignoring for the moment all the hundreds of thousands of words English has adopted from all the other languages in the world.]

So what? I hear you think. Well, just as the sounds of words have different qualities, so do the words derived from Old English and from

Latin. Words that are Old English in origin are short, blunt and down-to-earth; words derived from Latin or from Latin through French are generally longer and sound more formal. Take a simple example: house, residence, domicile. *House* comes from Old English; *residence* from Latin through French and *domicile* direct from Latin. Of course, if you invited your friends round to your residence, they would probably think you were sounding rather fancy – but that is the whole point. We associate words of Latinate origin with formality and elegance and sometimes poets might use words conscious of the power and associations that they have. Where a poet has used largely Latinate vocabulary it creates a special effect and there are poems in the Anthology where I have pointed this feature out. Equally, the down to earth simplicity of words of English origin can be robust and strong.

Alliteration is a technique that is easy to recognize and is used by many poets and writers to foreground their work. It can exist, of course, in any language. However, it seems to have appealed to writers in English for many centuries. Before 1066 when the Normans invaded and introduced French customs and culture, poetry was widely written in a language we now call Old English, or Anglo Saxon. Old English poetry did not rhyme. How was it patterned then? Each line had roughly the same number of syllables, but what was more important was that each line had three or four words that alliterated. Alliterative poetry continued to be written in English until the 14th century and if you look at these phrases drawn from everyday English speech I think you can see that it has a power even today: busy as a bee, cool as a cucumber, good as gold, right as rain, cheap as chips, dead as a doornail, kith and kin, hearth and home, spick and span, hale and hearty. Alliteration can also be found in invented names. Shops: Coffee Corner, Sushi Station, Caribou Coffee, Circuit City. Fictional characters: Peter Pan, Severus Snape, Donald Duck, Mickey Mouse, Nicholas Nickleby, Humbert Humbert, King Kong, Peppa Pig. The titles of films and novels: *Pride and Prejudice, Sense and Sensibility, Debbie Does Dallas, House on Haunted Hill, Gilmour Girls, V for Vendetta, A Christmas Carol, As Good as it Gets, The Witches of Whitby,*

The Wolf of Wall Street. Alliteration is an easy way to make words and phrases memorable.

So what? Well, as you read the poems and see alliteration being used, I think it is helpful to bear in mind that alliteration is not some specialized poetic technique, but is part of the fabric of everyday English too and it is used in everyday English for the same reasons that it is used by poets – to make the words more memorable.

An Approach to Poetry

This next bit may only be relevant if you are studying the poems for the first time and it is an approach that I use in the classroom. It works well and helps students get their bearing when they first encounter a poem. These are the Five Ws. They are not my idea, but I use them in the classroom all the time. They are simply five questions which are a starting point, a way of getting into the poem and a method of approaching an understanding of it. With some poems some of the answers to the questions are more important than others; with some poems these questions and our answers to them will not get us very far at all – but it is where we will start. I will follow this model with each commentary. They are also a good way to approach the unseen poem. The five questions to ask of each poem you read are:

- Who?

- When?

- Where?

- What?

- Why?

WHO? Who is in the poem? Whose voice the poem uses? This is the first and most basic question. In many poems the poet speaks as themselves, but sometimes they are ventriloquists – they pretend to be someone else. So first of all we must identify the voice of the poem. We must ask ourselves to whom the poem is addressed. It isn't always right to say – the reader; some poems are addressed to a particular individual. And, of course, there may well be other people mentioned in the poem itself. Some poetry is quite cryptic, so who 'you' and 'they' are in a poem make a crucial difference to the way we interpret it. Why are poems 'cryptic'? Well, one reason is that they use language in a very compressed way – compressed perhaps because of the length of each line or the decision to use rhyme.

WHEN? When was the poem written and when is it set? This is where context is important. We know our context: we are reading the poem now, but when the poem was written and when the poem is set (not always the same, by any means) is crucial to the way we interpret it. The gender or background of the poet might be important, the society they were living in, the circumstances which led them to write the poem – all these things can be crucial to how we interpret the poem.

WHERE? Where is the poem set? Where do the events described in the poem take place? With some poems this question is irrelevant; with others it is absolutely vital – it all depends on the poem. In the Anthology you will find some poems which depend on some understanding of where they are set for them to work; you will find other poems where the location is not specified or is irrelevant or generalized – again it depends on the poem.

WHAT? This means what happens in a poem. Some poems describe a place; some describe a particular moment in time; some tell a story; some have a story buried beneath their surface; some make statements – some may do several or all of these things at once. They are all potentially different, but what happens is something is very basic and should be grasped before you can move on to really appreciate a poem. Very often I have kept this section really short, because it is only when you start to look closely at language that you fully understand what is going.

WHY? This is the hardest question of all and the one with a variety of possible answers, depending on your exact view of the poem in question. I like to think of it asking ourselves 'Why did the poet write this poem?' Or what is the overall message or emotional impact of this poem? To answer it with every poem, we need to look at all the other questions, the way the poet uses language and its effect on us, and try to put into words the tone of the voice of the poem and the poem's overall impact. Students in the classroom often seem puzzled by my asking them to discuss the poem's tone. But it boils down to this - if you were reading the poem out loud, what tone of voice would you use? What is the mood or atmosphere of the poem? Does the poet, or whoever the poet is pretending to be, have a particular attitude to what he or she is writing about? Answering these questions helps us discuss the tone of the poem. But you may not agree with everybody else about this and this is good: through disagreement and discussion, our understanding of what we read is sharpened. In the commentaries on each poem in this Anthology this question 'Why?' is answered at the very end of each commentary, because it is only after looking closely at the poet's use of language, form and structure that we can begin to answer it. If you feel you know the poem well enough, you might just use the section 'Why?' for each poem as a quick reminder of what its main message is. For all the poems the 'Why?' section consists of a series of bullet points which attempt to give you the words to express what the poem's main point is.

A Word of Warning

This book and the commentaries on individual poems that follow are full of words to do with literature – the technical devices such as metaphor, simile, oxymoron. These are the vocabulary to do with the craft of writing and it is important that you understand them and can use them with confidence. It is the same as using the word *osmosis* in Biology or *isosceles* in Maths. However, in the examination, it is absolutely pointless to pick out a technique unless you can something vaguely intelligent about its effect – the effect is vital! The examiner will know when a poet is using alliteration and does not need you to point it out;

the sort of writing about poetry that consists of picking out technical devices and saying nothing about their effect or linking them in some meaningful way to the subject matter is worthless. I will suggest, in each commentary, what the effect might be, but we can generalize and say that all techniques with words are about making the poem memorable in some away – and this 'making something memorable' is also about foregrounding language. Language that is foregrounded means that is different from normal everyday language and that it draws attention to itself by being different – it would be like if we all went round every day and tried to use a metaphor and alliteration in everything that we said or if we tried speaking in rhyme all day – people would notice!

Warming Up

Before we look at any of the poems from the anthology, I want to briefly examine two poems to give you a taste of the approach that will be followed throughout the rest of the book. So we will start by looking at two completely different poems. I am not going to subject either to a full analysis, but I will demonstrate with both poems some crucial ways of reading poetry and give you some general guidance which will stand you in good stead when we deal with the poems in the anthology itself. This is not meant to confuse you, but to help. I cannot stress enough that these two poems are not ones that you will be assessed on. They are my choice – and I would use the same method in the classroom – introducing a class very slowly to poetry and 'warming up' for the anthology by practising the sorts of reading skills which will help with any poem. Besides, you may find the method valuable in your preparation for answering on the unseen poem in the exam.

Here is the first poem we will consider – one of the most famous love poems in the English Language – Sonnet 116 by William Shakespeare:

SONNET 116

Let me not to the marriage of true minds

22

Admit impediments. Love is not love
Which alters when it alteration finds,
Or bends with the remover to remove:
O no; it is an ever-fixed mark,
That looks on tempests, and is never shaken;
It is the star to every wandering bark,
Whose worth's unknown, although his height be taken.
Love's not Time's fool, though rosy lips and cheeks
Within his bending sickle's compass come;
Love alters not with his brief hours and weeks,
But bears it out even to the edge of doom.
   If this be error and upon me proved,
    I never writ, nor no man ever loved.

Context

Shakespeare is the most famous writer England has ever produced and his plays are known throughout the world. 'Sonnet 116' by William Shakespeare is part of a sonnet sequence of 154 sonnets – also known as a sonnet cycle. Readers have commented that in the sonnets as a whole, Shakespeare covers every aspect of arguably the most important and strongest human emotion – love - as well as our most powerful instinct – sexual desire and the whole range of what happens in what we now call human relationships. Unlike Shakespeare's plays (most of which were unpublished during his lifetime), the sonnets were published in 1609. What does this tell us? We are not entirely sure: it is generally felt that it shows that poetry was held in higher regard than writing plays, so perhaps Shakespeare published the sonnets to achieve fame and wealth; there is also the fact that in Shakespeare's era there were no copyright laws – so once a play was published, there was nothing to stop any theatre putting a play on without giving the writer any performance fees.

Of the 154 sonnets some are very famous and appears in many anthologies. These very famous ones are well-known by the general public too: in the past, BBC Radio 4 has sometimes run public surveys to discover the nation's favourite poem or the nation's favourite love poem and Shakespeare's sonnets are frequently voted into the top ten. If you like 'Sonnet 116', then you might like to read some of his others. They are readily available on-line and are known by their number and the first line:

Sonnet 18 – Shall I compare thee to a summer's day?

Sonnet 29 – When in disgrace with Fortune and men's eyes

Sonnet 55 – Not marble or the gilded monuments

Sonnet 57 – Being your slave what should I do?

Sonnet 71 – No longer mourn for me when I am dead

Sonnet 91 – Some glory in their birth, some in their skill

Sonnet 129 – The expense of spirit in a waste of shame

Sonnet 130 – My mistress' eyes are nothing like the sun

Because so little is known about Shakespeare's private life, there has been endless speculation about who the sonnets are addressed to – but none of this speculation helps us get any closer to the individual sonnets and their meaning and impact. Personally I find it of no interest whatsoever, because for me the words are what make the sonnets memorable and worth reading now – over four hundred years since they were first published.

'Sonnet 116' is often used in modern marriage services (nowadays some churches allow couples considerable freedom in choosing some of the words they use during the service) and I have even seen cards for sale which reproduce the words of the sonnet – these cards are intended to be sent to people who are getting married. The whole sonnet presents a love that is steadfast and loyal and unchanging in the face of other changes. We will look closely at the language and tone of the sonnet, but also consider a deeper and darker interpretation.

impediments – obstacles.

or...remove – or ends when one person leaves or stops the relationship.

ever-fixèd – permanent, not moving.

bark – ship.

time's fool – the fool of time, subject to time and aging.

bending sickle – a scythe and its curved shape; the Grim Reaper carries a sickle; sickles an scythes are long-handled tools used for chopping down tall crops or weeds; here it is used metaphorically – Time chops us down because we succumb to age and finally death.

compass – range.

bears it out – endures it.

doom – Doomsday, the end of the world in Christian mythology, the day of Final Judgement when Christ will come to earth again and decide who goes to Heaven and who to Hell. Shakespeare uses this to suggest that love will last forever – until the end of time or the end of the world.

Who? The voice of the poet – but the commentary that follows suggests the implied presence of other people.

When? The sonnets were published in 1609, but most scholars believe that Shakespeare began to write them in the 1590s. Within the poem no particular time is specified.

Where? No particular place is specified, so the location does not seem important.

What? Shakespeare states that true love will never change and then explores this assertion through a series of images in order to prove or demonstrate that love will never change.

Commentary

The opening sentence of the sonnet is justly famous: the recurrence of the letter *m* which both alliterates and is within certain words and the way the first line runs on into the second

Let me not to the marriage of true minds

Admit impediments

creates a gentle, calm, mellifluous tone which is appropriate to the sense: assonance on the letter / allows creates euphony, which is all enhanced by the enjambment. The next sentence too

Love is not love

Which alters when it alteration finds.

is often quoted on its own and offered as a universal truth: true love never changes no matter what happens. This second sentence is memorable not just because of the sentiment but because of the words: the repetition of the word *love* as well as *alter/ alteration* and the soft sounds of the letter / and *w* and *f*. So far the sonnet is quite clearly concerned with marriage and *alters* is a pun on what we find at the eastern end of a church the altar. *Impediment* too is a word, a very important word, in the Church of England marriage service. In the marriage service the priest says to the congregation, before the couple exchange their vows of marriage:

Does anyone know of any just cause or impediment why these two should not be joined together in holy matrimony?

Impediment here means an obstacle. At this point in the service, centuries ago, this was the moment when someone in the congregation could mention an obstacle – such one of the couple being already married or promised to someone else or below the legal age to marry or whatever. The final line of the quatrain continues this pattern of repetition – *remover/ remove.*

The second quatrain introduces new images in an effort to define what love is. Line 5 begins with a dramatic exclamation – *O no* – and then introduces a metaphor based on ships and navigation. Love is *ever-fixèd*: it never changes and can endure the fury of tempests without being shaken; love is like a star that guides sailors who would otherwise be lost (*wandering*) and they measure the height of the star (love) even before they understand whether the star will help them navigate. Shakespeare uses assonance – *star* assonates with the rhyme words *bark* and *mark* – and *whose worth's unknown* – repeats the same sound with *o* – which alos goes back to the exclamation at the start of the quatrain. This creates a sort of aural harmony even though he is writing about potentially dangerous things – tempests, and ships that are lost.

The third quatrain changes the line of thought again. It starts with a bold statement – *Love's not Time's fool*; Shakespeare means that true love will not alter even though time changes our physical appearance as we age. Time destroys *rosy lips and cheeks*. Not the consonance on *c* in *sickle's compass come*. Line 11 deliberately echoes the opening quatrain with its use of *alters*. The whole quatrain is held together not just by sense and subject matter and rhyme, but also alliteration – *bending, brief, but bears*. The final line says that love will last until Doomsday, the end of time.

The sonnet ends with an assertive couplet. Shakespeare states that if he is wrong – that if love is impermanent or transitory then it follows that he, the poet, never wrote a word and no human being ever really loved.

This poem is usually read as a definition of love or true love: an emotion that survives time and tempests, that will never change, no matter what happens. This is why it is so popular in connection with marriages – it serves, people think, as a vow of love that will last forever. Perhaps its power has a lot to do with its sounds: we have noted the clever use of repetition; the euphony created by the soft consonants in the opening quatrain; and, perhaps, its appeal has something to do with Shakespeare's straightforward imagery of stars and ships, rosy cheeks, death personified with his bending sickle. However, a closer reading will show that there is another possibility, another way to interpret this very famous poem.

Remember that in the first sentence Shakespeare had said he was not going to admit impediments – he is going to say nothing at this point of the marriage service. This suggests that Shakespeare is writing about the marriage of someone else and asserting that he still loves that person and his love will never change, despite the fact that they are marrying someone else and not him. It is ironic, isn't it, that the sonnet is so often used in marriage services: this is a poem about the end of a relationship – a relationship that is ending because one of the people involved in the relationship is getting married. Consequently, the speaker's feelings are of sadness and a sense of betrayal, but they are controlled by the strict form of the sonnet which helps to restrain the terrible sadness the speaker feels.

In the light of this reading of the poem, the poem's imagery still fits with what I wrote earlier in the summary, but some of the images take on a darker, sadder tone and atmosphere. The simile involving the *wandering bark* works as a simile, but it might also suggest Shakespeare's emotional state now that his former lover has rejected him to marry someone else – he is like a ship drifting. Love that bears it out until the edge of doom, means a love that will never die and will keep going until Doomsday, but that word *doom* perhaps suggests the terrible sadness that Shakespeare feels at the end of the relationship: in a sense it is almost like the end of the world for him. *Bears it out* suggests a determination to keep going despite the heartbreak he feels – and he does, in a sense, keep going, because the sonnet reaches its conclusion.

Why?

This world-famous poem

- offers a definition of love which many readers have comforting and inspiring.

- asserts that true love lasts forever and will endure absence and time and even death.

- uses simple repetition and wonderfully crafted combinations of sound to create euphony.

BUT it might also be read as

- a poem full of heartbreak and sadness at the loss of a loved one who marries someone else.

Here is the second poem that we will look at as an unseen:

The Sick Rose

O rose, thou art sick!
  The invisible worm,
That flies in the night,
  In the howling storm,

Has found out thy bed   5
  Of crimson joy,
And his dark secret love
  Does thy life destroy

thou – you

thy - your

Who? The voice of the poet, the invisible worm, a rose.

When? In the night during a storm.

Where? Hard to say... in the bed of the rose.

What? Just using what we know from the poem, we can say that an invisible worm discovers the dark secret love of the rose and destroys it during a storm.

29

It is obvious that this method will not get us very far with this type of poem or, at least, will not get us beyond a superficial interpretation of what it means.

What can we say with any certainty about this poem? Its mood is sinister. It is night-time and there is a howling storm. An invisible worm has found out where the rose has its bed and is coming to take its life. *Found out* suggest that the bed needs to be hidden. Paradoxically, although the worm is going to destroy the life of the rose, the worm has a *dark secret love* for the rose: this is now especially disturbing – a love which is dark and secret and which is destructive of life. Not only is it night and, therefore, dark, but the love of the worm is also dark and secret and destructive. We expect love to be a positive emotion which brings good things to our lives.

When faced with this poem many readers want to interpret the poem symbolically – otherwise it becomes a poem about horticulture. The poem is full of words that we associate with love - *rose, bed, joy, love.* In addition, in our culture sending someone roses, especially red roses, is a token of love. But this is a love which has gone wrong and is destructive. Many readers also find the shape of the worm rather phallic – suggestive of the penis. Think of all the types of love which might be considered 'wrong' or destructive. This is the list I came up with, but I am sure you can think of many others:

- Love for someone who does not love you back.

- Love for someone who is already married or in a relationship.

- Love which cannot be expressed.

- Love that transmits disease through unprotected sex.

- Love between two people from different religions.

- Love which is against the law.

- Love which is unwanted by the person you love.

- Love between two people of different class backgrounds.

- Love between two people of the same gender.

- Love or sexual expressions of love which are condemned by the church or by religious doctrine or law.

- Love which is possessive and selfish.

The point of this list is really to show that Blake's power of compression suggests a love that has gone wrong and leaves us to interpret it. To say that 'The Sick Rose' is about any one of the situations listed above would be totally wrong; to say that it suggests them all and encompasses them all, suggests the power of Blake's writing.

If you remember that the rose is the national symbol of England, then this poem becomes even more than a poem about love gone wrong – it becomes (perhaps) a poem about the state of England and a warning that it will soon be destroyed. You don't have to identify exactly what or who the worm is – the poem does that for you: the worm is destructive and capable of killing – it is a symbol of ALL the things Blake hated in his society. Blake's point is that the rose is sick and is about to be destroyed by sinister, invisible powers.

Finally, if you need any proof of Blake's power to compress meaning, just look at how many words I have used in an attempt to give meaning to his words: Blake uses (including the title) only thirty-seven! This is part of the poem's power and art – that is uses powerful words and imagery from which we can extract a multitude of meanings.

Why? This astonishingly compressed and darkly evocative poem is

- a protest about the England that Blake lived in.

- a protest about the way the church and society saw certain types of love as wrong.

- a warning that love – or what we call love- can be destructive if it is not fulfilled.

- a plea for tolerance and inclusion for those who conventional morality condemns.

Endings

This may seem like an obvious point, one hardly worth drawing attention to, but you have seen from the poems discussed above that the endings of poem are absolutely vital and crucial to their overall effect. In 'The Sick Rose' the final word – *destroy* – carries threat and menace. You will find in many of the poems in the Anthology the ending – the final stanza, the final line, the final sentence, even sometimes the final word – changes what has gone before and forces us to see things differently. So be aware of this as you read and as you revise. When you are writing about poems, the way they end and the emotional conclusion they achieve is a simple way to compare and contrast them. It may not be easy to express what it is exactly that they do achieve, but make sure you write something about the endings, because the endings are often the key to the whole poem. Remember – a poem (like a song) is an emotional journey and the destination, the ending, is part of the overall message, probably its most important part.

'When We Two Parted' – George Gordon, Lord Byron

Context

Byron was the ideal of the Romantic poet, gaining notoriety for his scandalous private life and being described by one contemporary as 'mad, bad and dangerous to know'. George Gordon Noel, sixth Baron Byron, was born on 22 January 1788 in London. His father died when he was three, with the result that he inherited his title from his great uncle in 1798.

Byron spent his early years in Aberdeen, and was educated at Harrow School and Cambridge University. In 1809, he left for a two-year tour of a number of Mediterranean countries. He returned to England in 1811, and in 1812 the first two cantos of 'Childe Harold's Pilgrimage' were published. Byron became famous overnight. His other works of this period 'The Corsair' and 'Hebrew Melodies' sold very well and Byron became a celebrity in fashionable society and the toast of London society. There is a case for thinking of him as the first celebrity poet.

In 1814, Byron's half-sister Augusta gave birth to a daughter, almost certainly Byron's. The following year Byron married Annabella Milbanke, with whom he had a daughter, his only legitimate child. The couple separated in 1816, in controversial circumstances – Byron being accused by his wife of 'unnatural practices'.

The furore over his marriage and his tangled love life led London society to shun him. Facing mounting pressure as a result of his failed marriage, scandalous affairs and huge debts, Byron left England in April 1816 and never returned. He spent the summer of 1816 at Lake Geneva with Percy Bysshe Shelley, his wife Mary and Mary's half-sister Claire Clairmont, with whom Byron had a daughter.

Byron travelled on to Italy, where he was to live for more than six years. In 1819, while staying in Venice, he began an affair with Teresa Guiccioli, the wife of an Italian nobleman. It was in this period that Byron wrote some of his most famous works, including 'Don Juan' (1819-1824).

In July 1823, Byron left Italy to join the Greek insurgents who were fighting a war of independence against the Ottoman Empire. On 19 April 1824 he died from fever at Missolonghi, in modern day Greece. His death was mourned throughout Britain. His body was brought back to England and buried at his ancestral home in Nottinghamshire.

sever – to cut through

knell – the bell that is sounded when someone has died.

rue - regret

Who? Byron (whom we assume to be the speaker in the poem) and an unnamed lady with whom he had an affair – often thought to be Lady Frances Wedderburn Webster. The poem is addressed to his former lover.

When? The poem was first published in 1816. Byron uses the present tense, but also shifts to the past tense in writing about their relationship and the way it ended.

Where? No specific location.

What? Byron laments the ending of the relationship and claims it still has the power to affect him on a deep emotional level.

Commentary

Byron is reflecting in poetry on a relationship that failed. The lovers have parted in 'silence and tears' and their separation has lasted for years: they have been severed 'for years'. At the time of their parting his lover's cheek grew cold and her kiss even colder; the last two lines of the first stanza show that the speaker still feels sorrow and anguish over their parting, feelings that still consume him in the present:

Truly that hour foretold

Sorrow to this.

When they parted the speaker felt the morning dew 'chill on my brow' and the pain of parting is something he feels even now:

It felt like a warning

Of what I feel now.

The third stanza introduces a mystery. He accuses his former lover of having broken all her vows and states that her fame is 'light' – not good: it implies that breaking her vows has led to a loss of reputation and social scandal. The speaker hears his lover's name spoken and he shares 'in its shame'. However, it is not made completely clear what that shame is nor why the speaker should share in it.

When his lover's name is mentioned in his hearing it is like a 'knell in mine ear'. However, no one knew of their relationship:

They know not that I knew thee,

Who knew thee too well.

How can you know someone too well? Perhaps their intimacy has been so intense that it pains him to think of what he has lost; alternatively, perhaps the poet knew she would break her vows. Byron ends the verse asserting through repetition how deeply he regrets the end of their relationship, so much so that he cannot describe his feelings in words:

Long, long shall I rue thee,

Too deeply to tell.

The final stanza's first two lines are bound together by alliteration on the second word of each line:

In secret we met,

In silence I grieve —

And the 'we' of the first line balances the 'I' of the second; the first line is in the past tense – the second line in the present. Byron's feelings of sadness are that his former lover could forget him ('thy heart could forget') and that she has in some way deceived him ('Thy spirit deceive'). In the final four lines Byron states that if they should meet now after so many years apart he would greet her 'With silence and tears', showing that the pain of the ending of the relationship continues and verbally reminding us of the second line of the poem – nothing has changed since the day they parted. Byron still feels intense sorrow at their parting.

Byron uses a strict rhyme scheme and generally each line has two stressed syllables. He chooses words that are mainly monosyllabic. The short words, the short lines and the regular rhyme scheme (ABABCDCD) give Byron a formal control over the poem, but paradoxically hint at turbulent emotions below the surface which are controlled and held back by the formal aspects of the construction of the poem. This paradox, in its turn, means that the poem we are left with is deeply felt and moving – because the words, lines and rhyme scheme are so tightly controlled. It's almost as if Byron cannot trust himself to be more expansive or his emotions would burst forth in an unrestrained muddle… so the control he exercises in the poem is a deliberate ploy to help restrain and control intense emotions.

Overall this is a sad and bitter poem, and one that is not really concerned with Byron's lover at all: it is more concerned with her effect on him and the enduring sense of loss he feels at their separation.

Although first published in 1816, Byron said that he wrote the poem in 1808 in order to protect the identity of the woman he was writing about. Lady Francis Wedderburn Webster was linked romantically to the Duke of Wellington, and poem describes Byron's emotional state at the end of his secret relationship with Lady Frances and her rejection of him for the Duke of Wellington. Her affair with the Duke scandalized society, but Byron in the poem is scrupulous in keeping her identity a secret.

A Romantic Poem?

The relatively simple diction and the very simple form – only two stressed syllables per line make this a typically Romantic poem. It is also Romantic because it deals with intimate, intense personal feelings. These characteristics mark it out as different from the poetry that immediately preceded it.

Byron's 'When We Two Parted':

- is a poem of intense emotion and heart-break;

- uses a short metre and relatively simple vocabulary to express his feelings – even claiming at one point that he cannot find the words he needs;

- the rigid control of the rhyme scheme and metre suggest passionate feelings which are being kept under control;

- uses the past and present tenses in a masterful way – to suggest the effect of their initial break up and its continuing source of pain to Byron.

'Love's Philosophy' – Percy Shelley

Context

Percy Bysshe Shelley was born in 1792 and drowned in a boating accident just before his 30th birthday in 1822. He lived in turbulent times: the French Revolution had begun in 1789 and in Britain the Industrial Revolution was changing the country in deep and lasting ways. Shelley was quite a rebel – and was a political radical. He sympathized with the ideas behind the French Revolution and wanted to see greater change in Britain – more democracy, more freedom, less oppression. You should remember that although Britain was an enormously wealthy nation (because of the Industrial Revolution and the huge expanse of the British Empire), the majority of the population lived in appalling poverty and most adults did not have the vote – the right to vote was limited to those who owned a certain amount of property and was, therefore, limited to a tiny minority of adult males. It was not until 1928 that all men (regardless of what they owned) were able to vote. This poem, however, has no political resonances.

fountains – natural springs of water, not man-made fountains.

mingle – mix together.

clasp – embrace

disdained – scorned, rejected, looked down upon.

Who? The speaker (whom we may assume is Shelley) attempts to persuade a woman to love him and to kiss him.

When? The poem was published in 1820.

Where? There is no specific location.

What? The poet uses a series of examples from nature of things which mix, mingle or join together in order to persuade the woman to love him.

Commentary

This short and simple poem has a rather grand title – 'Love's Philosophy' – and we will see by the end of this commentary that Shelley's ideas do have a basis in a very serious view of humanity's relationship with nature and the Romantic view of nature.

The first stanza begins by listing things in nature that are intimately connected:

The fountains mingle with the river

And the rivers with the ocean.

The winds of heaven mix for ever

With a sweet emotion.

The opening stanza avoids using any plosive consonants – there is a preponderance of 'm's and 'w's and the gentle tone is enhanced by the feminine rhyme which Shelley uses in the first seven lines of the first stanza. The effect is also enhanced by Shelley's use of personification which leads naturally to his conclusion (he is, after all writing a poem to persuade a woman to love him):

Nothing in the world is single,

All things by a law divine

In another's being mingle —

So why not I with thine?

The feminine line endings continue until the final line of the stanza which ends on a clear masculine ending – 'thine'. Shelley is arguing that there is a universal law that everything in nature is connected and the personification in the first verse is carried by the verbs 'mix' and 'mingle' and 'mingle' is repeated in line 1 and line 7.

The second stanza continues with more examples from nature, but Shelley's vocabulary is more loving and romantic. Personification is used throughout as it is in the first stanza, but the verbs are more passionate and more obviously connected to romantic love:

See the mountains <u>kiss</u> high heaven.

And the waves <u>clasp</u> one another.

'Kiss and 'clasp' will be repeated at the end of the stanza and in the first half of the second stanza Shelley continues to use feminine rhyme, which makes the poem more tentative and less forceful as befits a persuasive poem. However, line 13 marks a change to masculine rhymes and the tone of the poem becomes more confident as a result:

And the sunlight clasps the earth,

And the moonbeams kiss the sea —

What is all this sweet work worth,

If thou kiss not me?

Interestingly, both stanzas end with a rhetorical question and the final line of each stanza is made up of monosyllabic words – as if implying that the answer to the question is simple – the lovers should follow all the examples that Shelley gives from nature and kiss and clasp one another. This is Shelley's argument: we are surrounded by pairs of things which mingle and kiss and we should follow their example. His use of a regular stanza enhances the notion that this is a logical argument: two stanzas of eight lines each with a matching rhyme scheme – ABABCDCD.

All the examples Shelley uses from nature are personified and in all of the examples he sees examples of love, harmony and intimacy. This could be seen as a sort of extended example of pathetic fallacy where one's natural surroundings reflect one's feelings and emotions.

Some readers are critical of Shelley's title, arguing that the poem does not set out a philosophy at all. However, if we look at Romantic ideas about the world and science, we will find a close correlation between the poem's presentation of the natural world and the principles of Romantic science.

Romanticism had four basic principles: the original unity of man and nature in a Golden Age; the subsequent separation of man from nature and the fragmentation of human faculties; the interpretability of the history of the universe in human, spiritual terms; and the possibility of salvation through the contemplation of nature.

To Romantics, science must not bring about any split between nature and man. Romantics believed in the intrinsic ability of mankind to understand nature and its phenomena. They preferred not to dissect information as some insatiable thirst for knowledge and did not advocate what they viewed as the manipulation of nature, but rather mankind's acceptance of it.

Natural science, according to the Romantics, involved rejecting mechanical metaphors in favour of organic ones; in other words, they chose to view the world as composed of living beings with sentiments, rather than objects that merely function. Sir Humphry Davy, a prominent Romantic thinker, said that understanding nature required "an attitude of admiration, love and worship, a personal response." He believed that knowledge was only attainable by those who truly appreciated and respected nature. Self-understanding was an important aspect of Romanticism. It had less to do with proving that man was capable of understanding nature (through his budding intellect) and therefore controlling it, and more to do with the emotional appeal of connecting himself with nature and understanding it through a harmonious co-existence. Shelley's poem certainly sees humanity aspiring to a harmonious existence with the natural world. His consistent personification and the organic harmony he asserts is present in nature are also completely in tune with the Romantic view of the natural world and humanity – an organic, mutually-supportive relationship.

A Romantic Poem?

Let us be clear about one thing: this is NOT a Romantic poem because it is about love. It is, however, a Romantic poem because it deals with intimate, personal feelings and because (as we have just discussed above) it presents nature and humanity's relationship with it in a way that is in complete harmony with the Romantic view of nature and of science.

Shelley's 'Love's Philosophy':

- is a simple poem of persuasion;

- personifies nature throughout and links it to human behaviour;

- presents a view of nature and the natural world which has its roots in the Romantic view of science;

- uses simple language and repetition to present Shelley's ideas.

'Porphyria's Lover' – Robert Browning

Context

Robert Browning was born in 1812 and became one of the most famous English poets of the Victorian era. He was married to Elizabeth Barrett Browning who was a semi-invalid with an over-protective father. The couple were married in secret and then went to live in Italy. Browning's best work is often set in the past and he was a master of the dramatic monologue, in which the imagined speaker of the poem reveals their innermost thoughts and feelings, often going on to uncover uncomfortable truths about themselves.

porphyria – a rare disorder of the blood that may cause mental, nervous or skin problems.

vex – annoy, anger.

soiled – dirty, unclean.

dissever – to separate, to part in two.

oped – opened.

tress – a long lock of hair.

Who? The poem is a dramatic monologue spoken by the male lover of Porphyria.

When? One dark stormy might. Browning uses the weather as a pathetic fallacy for the turbulent human emotions in the cottage.

Where? In an isolated cottage.

What? The speaker, without a word of explanation or regret, tells of Porphyria's visit to him and his subsequent murder of her. The speaker spends the night alone with the body of his dead lover.

Commentary

'Porphyria's Lover' by Robert Browning dramatizes the conflicts between social pressures and romantic love; the tension between female submissiveness and the male urge to possess, to control and to act; the tension between momentary pleasure and the human need to preserve and keep that transitory pleasure; and the tension between strong religious faith and religious doubt.

In 'Porphyria's Lover' Browning presents a speaker who is insane. The poem was originally published in 1836 in the London journal *Monthly Repository* (Hawlin, 44) and was paired with another poem with an identical rhyme scheme, metre, line length and overall length (Ryals, 166). The paired poems were printed under the title 'Madhouse Cells' and the other poem, 'Johannes Agricola in Meditation', shares a similar preoccupation to 'Porphyria's Lover' – what Ryals calls the desire or will for 'total possession of another person' (166).

The poem is a dramatic monologue – a type of poem that Browning would continue to write throughout his career, but in this early example the monologue seems to be addressed to the reader; later dramatic monologues, such as 'My Last Duchess' and 'Fra Lippo Lippi' where Browning developed the form by including within the poem other characters to whom the monologue is addressed (Ryals, 87). In 'Porphyria's Lover' the speaker is isolated in many ways as we will see. The speaker is recounting the events of the previous evening, so the poem is written after the main event of the poem (which Browning, as the poet, cleverly delays until line 42.). The speaker – the lover of

Porphyria – has a tender tone as he recounts the events of the previous evening: indeed, Hawlin comments that his 'whole perspective is… gentle or feminized' (46). However, the speaker is also mad, and the crucial event of the poem in line 42, throws his previous solicitude and apparent love and care for Porphyria into a dark and deadly ironic light.

Browning's monologues are frequently voiced by eccentrics, lunatics, or people under emotional stress. Their ramblings illustrate character by describing the interactions of an odd personality with a particularly telling set of circumstances. In both 'Porphyria's Lover' and 'My Last Duchess', Browning uses this mode of exposition to describe a man who responds to the love of a beautiful woman by killing her. Each monologue offers the speakers' reasons for the desired woman from subject to object: in 'My Last Duchess', the Duke may have jealously murdered his wife, but keeps a portrait of her behind a curtain so none can look upon her smile without his permission; in 'Porphyria's Lover', the persona wishes to stop time at a single perfect moment and so kills his lover and sits all night embracing her carefully arranged body. It should be noted that in 'My Last Duchess' the woman's murder is at best implied, while in 'Porphyria's Lover' it is described quite explicitly by the speaker. The unchanging rhythmic pattern may also suggest the persona's insanity.

The 'Porphyria' persona's romantic egotism leads him into all manner of monstrously selfish assumptions compatible with his own longings. He seems convinced that Porphyria wanted to be murdered, and claims 'No pain felt she' while being strangled, adding, as if to convince himself, 'I am quite sure she felt no pain.' He may even believe she enjoyed the pain, because he, her lover, inflicted it. When she's dead, he says she's found her 'utmost will,' and when he sees her lifeless head drooping on his shoulder, he describes it as a 'smiling rosy little head', possibly using the word 'rosy' to symbolise the red roses of love, or to demonstrate his delusion that the girl, and their relationship, are still alive. More likely, however, is the thought that blood returning to her face, after the strangulation, makes her cheeks 'rosy.' Her 'rosy little head' may also be a sly reference to the hymen; Porphyria leaves a 'gay feast' and comes in from the outside world wearing 'soiled gloves'; now her blue eyes, open in death, are 'without a stain.' The lover may also be a **fetishist**, indicated by the fact that he refers to her hair numerous times throughout the poem, and strangles her with it. He also refers to the 'shut bud that holds a bee' which backs up the view of it being a sexual fetish.

It is impossible to know the true nature of his relationship to Porphyria. An incestuous relationship has been suggested; Porphyria might be the speaker's mother or sister. Another possibility is that she is a former lover, now betrothed, or even married, to some other man. Alternatively, they may be divided by social class.

Other sources speculate that the lover might be impotent, disabled, sick, or otherwise inadequate, and, as such, unable to satisfy Porphyria. There is much textual evidence to support this interpretation: he describes himself as 'one so pale / for love of her, and all in vain.' At the beginning of the poem, the persona never moves; he sits passively in a cold, dark room, sadly listening to the storm until Porphyria comes through 'wind and rain', 'shuts the cold out and the storm,' and makes up his dying fire. Finally, she sits beside him, calls his name, places his arm around her waist, and puts his head on her shoulder; interestingly, she has to stoop to do this. She is active; he is passive – suggesting impotence perhaps. At the poem's midpoint, the persona suddenly takes action, strangling Porphyria, propping her body against his, and boasting that afterwards, *her* head lay on *his* shoulder.

In line with the persona's suggested weakness and sickness, other scholars take the word 'porphyria' literally, and suggest that the seductress embodies a disease, and that the persona's killing of her is a sign of his recovery. Porphyria, which usually involved delusional madness and death, was classified several years before the poem's publication; Browning, who had an avid interest in such pathologies, may well have been aware of the new disease, and used it in this way to express his knowledge.

Much has been made of the final line: 'And yet, God has not said a word!' Possibly, the speaker seeks divine approval for the murder. He may believe God has said nothing because He is satisfied with his actions. God may be satisfied because: He recognises that the persona's crime is the only way to keep Porphyria pure; or, because He doesn't think her life and death are important compared to the persona's. The persona may also be waiting in vain for some sign of God's approval. Alternatively, the line may represent his feelings of emptiness in the wake of his violence; Porphyria is gone, quiet descends, and he's alone. The persona may also be **schizophrenic**; he may be listening for a voice in his head, which he mistakes for the voice of God. It has also been postulated that this is Browning's statement of 'God's silence,' in which neither good nor bad acts are immediately recompensed by the deity.

The final line may also register the persona's sense of guilt over his crime. Despite his elaborate justifications for his act, he has, in fact, committed murder, and he expects God to punish him – or, at least, to take notice. The persona is surprised, perhaps a little uneasy, at God's continued silence. An alternative reading of the last line is to identify a slightly gleeful tone in it – confirming once again that the speaker is insane.

There is no doubt of his insanity; exactly why he kills Porphyria is open to debate and interpretation.

The poem is set in an isolated rural cottage: Browning implies this because Porphyria who has walked through a storm to meet her lover is completely wet and immediately takes off her 'dripping cloak and shawl' (line 11) and her 'soiled gloves' (line 12). Browning uses the storm as a pathetic fallacy in at least three ways: firstly, it is an effective contrast with the warmth and love within the cottage once Porphyria lights the fire and makes advances to her lover; secondly, it can be seen as Browning foreshadowing the later, violent events of the poem; and, thirdly, it might even be seen as symbolizing the tortured inner feelings of Porphyria's 'murderously jealous lover' (Hair & Kennedy, 88) – feelings which he keeps under careful control. Knoepflmacher argues that Browning presents very well the 'contrast between a cold outside world and a warm interior' (158) and Porphyria herself can be seen as 'the passionate outsider penetrating that interior who brings warmth to the immobile dreamer within' (158). However, this can be seen as an example of prolepsis, since, despite the speaker's self-delusional assertions, in death Porphyria's body will rapidly lose all its warmth.

The relationship between the two lovers is presented by Browning as a clandestine one, but one which Porphyria wants: she has, after all, braved a storm to visit her lover and the way she 'put my arm about her waist,/And made her smooth white shoulder bare' (lines 16 -17) clearly suggests that the relationship is sexual. It seems that Browning suggests that it has to be clandestine because Porphyria and her lover are from different classes: Martens asserts that the poem is essentially about a man's 'pathological love for a socially-superior woman' (39). Browning suggests this through the speaker's words: he says that Porphyria is 'too weak... from pride' (lines 22 & 24) – presumably a pride issuing from her social superiority and the disgrace she would suffer if her love for this man became known, and he goes on to say that she is 'too weak' (line 22) to allow her 'struggling passion free' (line 23) and 'give herself to me forever' (line 25), because she is socially bound by what the speaker dismisses as 'vainer ties' (line 24) – presumably her sense of responsibility to her family. Browning presents the speaker as being very distraught at this situation: it explains why he does not respond in line 15 when she calls him and he comments that, because he cannot have her forever or is dependent on her secret visits to him, it seems that his love for her is 'all in vain' (line 30). But passion prevails – Browning hints perhaps that they make love and, as they do so, the man notices how Porphyria is looking at him and realizes 'I knew/Porphyria worshipped me' (lines 33 -34). He goes on:' That moment she was mine, mine, fair,/Perfectly pure and good' (line 38). But it is only a moment of intense feeling and, given what Browning has suggested about the nature of their relationship and his dependence on her coming to him when she can and not when she or he both want, he decides to preserve the moment and strangles her with her own hair. The repeated 'mine, mine' in line 37 convey his extreme possessiveness and Knoepflmacher writes that 'by draining Porphyria of her life, he can assume... control' (160). This can easily be seen as symptomatic of the masculine desire to possess and control, the human desire to preserve forever a moment of happiness, and we might even see the speaker as rebelling against a rigid class system which keeps him and his lover apart. However, by killing Porphyria, Browning presents the insane speaker as having wholly abrogated all moral responsibility for his actions and acted in defiance of human law and morality.

Mirroring the speaker's desire for control, the poem's structure is highly controlled. On the page the poem looks highly regular and it is: Browning conveys his speaker's thoughts with a regular unvarying rhyme scheme which consists of units of six lines which rhyme ABABB, CDCDD and so on. This tightly-controlled and very regular rhyme scheme could be said to mirror the speaker's own need for control and his obsession with Porphyria; at the same time, despite the horrific nature of his crime, his speaking voice remains calm and untroubled – just as the poem is very formally and regularly structured. Hawlin (42) describes the rhyme scheme as 'assymetrical' – presumably meaning that we might expect the six line unit to rhyme like this – ABABAB – but the rhyme scheme that Browning has chosen with the fifth and sixth line rhyming with each other, means that in terms of rhyme, the six line unit turns back on itself – an attempt surely to accentuate the self-obsessed, inward-looking nature of the speaker. In other words, the speaker is concerned only with his own feelings, despite his apparent concern for Porphyria – (No pain felt she;/I am quite sure she felt no pain' (lines 42 – 43). As Bailey asserts, the speaker has a 'megalomaniac stance towards his lover' (53), and he is 'self-deceiving' (Hair & Kennedy, 88). This self-deception and the evidence of his insanity continues after Porphyria is dead: the speaker thinks that her eyes 'laughed... without a stain' (line 46) and that 'her cheek once more/Blushed bright beneath my burning kiss' (lines 48 -49).

Browning uses a lot of enjambment – twenty-two times in a poem of sixty lines - so that over a third of the lines run on and are not end-stopped. On the one hand, it could be said that this enjambment helps convey the impression of a real voice that is speaking, but there is perhaps another purpose: in so many lines the words and syntax break through the end of the line and this is a poem about a speaker who breaks accepted morality by committing murder. Furthermore, the lines which build up to and describe Porphyria's murder – lines 32 to 42 – use an excessive amount of enjambment which perhaps help to convey the speaker's frenzy, emphasize his breaking of the rules and quicken the rhythm of the poem to its climax, as well as imitating the speedy act of strangling his lover. Browning's use of heavy, full-stop caesuras is equally significant. He uses only two: one in line 15 after Prophyria 'sat down by my side/And called me.' (lines 14 – 15) – a caesura which is used to emphasize the speaker's lack of response to her; the second in line 42 after 'strangled her' – which again serves, for the reader, to emphasize the enormity of the crime he has committed. The caesura helps to foreground the act of murder. However, Browning presents the speaker as so delusional that he argues that in killing his lover he was doing what she would have wanted: he describes her head as 'so glad it has its utmost will' (line 54) and he claims in his insanity that his killing of her is 'her darling one wish' (line 58). The speaker's final observation – that on the subject of the murder 'God has not said a word!' (line 60) – certainly shows the speaker's contempt and insouciance towards religious diktats forbidding murder.

Browning's 'Porphyria's Lover' is a deeply disturbing poem, enhanced by the strict regularity of the rhyme scheme and the control that Browning exerts over it. What appears to be a passionate story of the secret tryst of two lovers turns into a tale of sudden and violent murder, and a crazed and deluded justification of it. Ryals states that 'there has been some disagreement as to whether the lover kills Porphyria because he loves her or hates her' (271): it could be argued that such a question is irrelevant because, love her or hate her, he seeks to possess her completely and forever. It can be seen that the poem raises other issues – the unfairness of the British class system, the habitual, historical male need to dominate and a growing scepticism about God – but these are overshadowed by the pathological and wholly solipsistic megalomania of the speaker.

Works Cited

Bailey, Suzanne. *Cognitive Style and Perceptual Difference in Browning's Poetry*. London: Routledge, 2010. Print.

Browning, Robert. 'Porphyria's Lover'. *Poetry Foundation*. Web. October 28th, 2013.

Hair, Donald S. & Kennedy, Richard S. *The Dramatic Imagination of Robert Browning: A Literary Life*. Columbia, Mi: University of Missouri Press, 2007. Print.

Hawlin, Stefan. *Robert Browning*. London: Routledge, 2012. Print.

Knoepflmacher, U. C. 'Projection of the Female Other: Romanticism, Browning and the Victorian Dramatic Monologue'. Pp. 147 – 168 in Claridge, Laura & Langland, Elizabeth (eds.). *Out of Bounds: Male Writers and Gendered Criticism*. Boston, Ma: University of Massachusetts Press, 1990. Print.

Martens, Britta. *Browning, Victorian Poetics and the Romantic Legacy: Challenging the Personal Voice*. London: Aldgate Publishing Ltd, 2011. Print.

Ryals, Clyde de L. *Robert Browning: The Poems and Plays of Robert Browning, 1833 – 1846*. Columbus, Oh: Ohio State University Press, 1983. Print.

In 'Porphyria's Lover' Browning:

- uses dramatic monologue to present a solipsistic, psychopathic maniac;

- to suggest an illicit love affair, perhaps caused by social differences;

- uses a rigid rhyme scheme and metre to suggest the speaker's confidence and rigidity of thinking, but also uses caesura brilliantly at key moments;

- presents an insane mind obsessed with full possession of his lover;

- in the poem presents possessive love as a life-denying force.

Further Reading

What follows is the poem that was paired with 'Porphyria's Lover' by Browning under the title 'Madhouse Cells': it is very different from 'Porphyria's Lover', but is worth reading because it shows Browning presenting another character who suffers from extreme solipsism and a psychopathic conviction that he is right. It is another portrait of an insane character.

'Johannes Agricola in Meditation' (1836)

The speaker believes in an extreme form of predestination, claiming that, since he's one of the elect, he can commit any sin without forfeiting his afterlife in heaven.

There's heaven above, and night by night
I look right through its gorgeous roof;
No suns and moons though e'er so bright
Avail to stop me; splendour-proof
I keep the broods of stars aloof:
For I intend to get to God,
For 't is to God I speed so fast,
For in God's breast, my own abode,
Those shoals of dazzling glory, passed,
I lay my spirit down at last.
I lie where I have always lain,
God smiles as he has always smiled;

Ere suns and moons could wax and wane,
Ere stars were thundergirt, or piled
The heavens, God thought on me his child;
Ordained a life for me, arrayed
Its circumstances every one
To the minutest; ay, God said
This head this hand should rest upon
Thus, ere he fashioned star or sun.
And having thus created me,
Thus rooted me, he bade me grow,
Guiltless for ever, like a tree
That buds and blooms, nor seeks to know
The law by which it prospers so:
But sure that thought and word and deed
All go to swell his love for me,
Me, made because that love had need
Of something irreversibly
Pledged solely its content to be.
Yes, yes, a tree which much ascend,
No poison-gourd foredoomed to stoop!
I have God's warrant, could I blend
All hideous sins, as in a cup,
To drink the mingled venoms up;
Secure my nature will convert
The draught to blossoming gladness fast:
While sweet dews turn to the gourd's hurt,
And bloat, and while they bloat it, blast,
As from the first its lot was cast.
For as I lie, smiled on, full-fed
By unexhausted power to bless,
I gaze below on hell's fierce bed,
And those its waves of flame oppress,
Swarming in ghastly wretchedness;
Whose life on earth aspired to be
One altar-smoke, so pure! -- to win
If not love like God's love for me,
At least to keep his anger in;
And all their striving turned to sin.
Priest, doctor, hermit, monk grown white

With prayer, the broken-hearted nun,
The martyr, the wan acolyte,
The incense-swinging child, -- undone
Before God fashioned star or sun!
God, whom I praise; how could I praise,
If such as I might understand,
Make out and reckon on his ways,
And bargain for his love, and stand,
Paying a price at his right hand?'

'Sonnet XXIX' – Elizabeth Barrett Browning

Context

 Elizabeth Barrett Browning was born into a wealthy family in 1806. At the age of 14 she suffered from a lung complaint and the following year damaged her spine in a riding accident; she was to be plagued with poor health for the rest of her life. Elizabeth had started to publish poetry anonymously and was starting to become famous. In 1838 her brother Edward drowned off the coast of Devon and for the next five years Elizabeth became a recluse, hardly leaving her bedroom in her father's house. However, she continued to write poetry and began a long correspondence with the poet Robert Browning, who began writing to her after reading her poems. Between 1844 and 1846 they wrote 574 letters to each other and finally ran away to Italy to get married. They had to flee to Italy because Elizabeth's father was violently opposed to the marriage. She and her father never spoke again and he disinherited her. Her health improved in Italy and she gave birth to a son in 1849. She died in her husband's arms in 1861.

'Sonnet XXIX' is from the sonnet cycle *Sonnets from the Portuguese* which she wrote during their correspondence and before their marriage. (*Sonnets from the Portuguese* is simply the title she chose – they are not translations and do not exist in Portuguese!). This sonnet cycle explores the development and growth of her love for Browning and, although she wrote many other poems, it is these sonnets for which she is mainly remembered today. What is interesting and rarely mentioned in guides like this, is that the earlier poems in the sonnet cycle were not as confident as 'Sonnet'. In the earlier sonnets she is afraid of the consequences of her love for Browning and unsure about her own feelings: 'Sonnet XXIX' is from the middle of the sonnet cycle and represents the achievement of a confident, mature love.

insphere – to encircle or surround

Who? The sonnet was written by Elizabeth Barrett Browning before she was married to Robert Browning. The poem is addressed to her future husband.

When? The poem was published in 1850 as part of a 44 sonnet cycle entitled 'Sonnets from the Portuguese'. Despite the title they are completely original and not based on any Portuguese poems at all. Within the poem there is no specific time.

Where? No specific location.

What? This is a highly personal poem and Barrett Browning describes her thoughts and feelings when she is not with her lover.

Commentary

The opening exclamation, emphasized by the heavy caesura, conveys Barrett Browning's excitement when she thinks about her lover and future husband. The enjambment between lines one and two and again between lines three and four add to the air of sheer excitement that she feels. The opening quatrain also introduces the central metaphor which runs throughout the poem: her lover is a tree and Barrett Browning's thoughts are like 'wild vines' that 'twine and bud' around the tree. This is an interesting metaphor: the word 'wild' suggests her passion and excitement, while the image of her lover as a tree suggests something strong, upright and dependable; the vines only exist because they can twine around the tree, suggesting that Barrett Browning is nothing without her lover. The tree also is clearly a phallic image, emphasizing her lover's masculinity. The central metaphor – because it is drawn from nature – also suggests that their love is natural as well as exciting and passionate. In line 3 she orders him to 'put out broad leaves', so that the trunk of the tree cannot be seen when the broad leaves mingle with her 'wild vines'. Again his strength is contrasted to her relative weakness: her vines (which use the tree as a support) are merely the 'straggling green'.

The second quatrain begins with a direct address to her lover – 'Yet, O my palm tree' – which continues the metaphor and with 'yet' suggests she is going to raise a contradiction to the opening quatrain. In lines 5, 6 and 7 she explains that having thoughts about him is a feeble substitute for actually being with him and the lines gain intensity from the enjambment which suggests impatience and passion at the same time. In line 7 she exclaims that he is 'dearer, better!' – and this is given added force by the strong caesura of the exclamation mark. She orders him with a series of imperatives:

Renew thy presence; as a strong tree should,

Rustle thy boughs and set thy trunk all bare

Barrett Browning does not have a traditional volta or turn in line 9 of this sonnet, but the long sentence which starts on line 7 changes the course of the thought and feeling in the sonnet. She wants all the 'bands of greenery' which 'insphere' him to 'drop heavily down' – so that there are no barriers between them. She uses images of violence and an exclamation to suggest the strength of her desire to see him and be with him: the greenery will be 'burst, shattered, everywhere!' The image of 'thy trunk all bare' has strong phallic overtones.

And why does she want all the greenery to be stripped away so that it drops 'heavily down'?

Because, in this deep joy to see and hear thee

And breathe within thy shadow a new air,

I do not think of thee – I am too near thee.

When they are together or when they will be together, she has no need to think of him as she is overwhelmed by his physical presence. The poem began with 'I think of thee', but ends with 'I do not think of thee' – an interesting reversal of words, caused by their finally being together.

Barrett Browning's father's opposition to her marriage to Robert Browning is important to remember. It was unusual in the early Victorian period for middle class women to defy their fathers as Barrett Browning did. Some readers have seen in the imagery of the greenery being 'burst' and 'shattered', the hope that they can be together and defy the wishes of her father. The image of breaking free from the 'vines' could be seen as a reference to the speaker breaking free from her father's domination. Barrett Browning's excitement, commitment and passion for her lover are clear throughout the sonnet.

Elizabeth Barrett Browning's 'Sonnet XXIX':

- is a fiercely passionate and excited poem about Barrett Browning's love for Robert Browning with strong sexual connotations;

- it follows the form of a Petrarchan sonnet with two quatrains and a sestet, but the speaker's exclamations and frequent use of enjambment convey her passion and excitement;

- uses an extended metaphor with Robert Browning as a solid, strong tree and Elizabeth as the leaves and vines that grow up the trunk of the tree;

- the metaphor has been 'shattered' in line 11 because thinking about him is a poor substitute for being with him – and the last three lines imagine their successful meeting and perhaps the consummation of their love. She has no need to think of him or to construct elaborate metaphors about their love, because they are together.

'Neutral Tones' – Thomas Hardy

Context

 Thomas Hardy (1840 – 1928) is best known as a novelist. He wrote 15 novels, most of which are set largely in Dorset and the surrounding counties, and which deal with the ordinary lives of ordinary people in stories in which they struggle to find happiness and love – often battling against fate or their own circumstances. His final two novels *Tess of the D'Urbervilles* (1891) and *Jude the Obscure* (1895) both portray sex outside marriage in a sympathetic way and there was such a hysterical public outcry about the novels that Hardy stopped writing fiction and devoted the rest of his life to poetry. Although much of his poetry reflects his interest in nature and ordinary things, this poem is also typical of his work in that it is intensely personal and may reflect the intense unhappiness he felt in his first marriage.

Neutral – this can refer to the landscape, drained of vivid colours, but can also refer to the lovers in the poem – who are presented as being completely indifferent to one another.

Tones – like 'neutral' above this can refer to colour (or the lack of it), but also to the mood of the former lovers.

chidden – this is the past of 'to chide'. To chide means to tell off or to reprimand. Here it is as though God had told off the white sun.

sod – turf, the earth with grass on it.

rove – wander.

bird-a-wing – a bird in flight.

curst - cursed

Who? There is no reason to assume that the speaker is not Hardy himself. His lover is with him in the poem and this is seen in Hardy's use of the third person plural – 'we'.

When? On a cold winter's day. Hardy wrote the poem in 1867 at the age of 27, but it was not published until 1898.

Where? In the countryside beside a pond.

What? Hardy is looking back with bitterness and intense sadness at the end of a relationship.

Commentary

This is a bitter and pessimistic poem about the break-up of a relationship – one which Hardy remembers vividly and which still causes him pain and anguish. As a 'break up' poem, it is hard to think of a better one in the English Language – unless it's Byron's 'When We Two Parted'. Hardy uses pathetic fallacy throughout the poem, so the details of the weather and the landscape match and mirror the emotions of the two lovers.

The first stanza sets the scene. It is a bleak winter's day and the speaker and his former lover are standing by a pond. The landscape seems stripped of all fertility and strength. There are a few grey ash leaves scattered about and the sun, source of heat and light and life, is 'white, as though chidden of God' – chidden for being 'white' and for not offering any heat or real light on this miserable day? The sod is starving just as this relationship is starved now of any real love or affection.

In the second stanza Hardy directly addresses his lover, the first line using parallelism – 'eyes on me/eyes that rove'. Her eyes are like eyes that wander over 'tedious riddles of years ago' – suggesting that the relationship has been going on for years but that it has become 'tedious' – monotonous and uninteresting – a long time ago. They exchange some words (which Hardy does not bother to use in the poem) and he writes that the words they exchange – 'lost the more by our love': the words they speak now are trivial and meaningless and are in contrast to the love they once felt for each other. They are dull and irrelevant now (lost the more) in comparison with the love they once enjoyed (our love).

Hardy begins the third stanza with a scathing and oxymoronic simile by writing:

The smile on your mouth was the deadest thing

Alive enough to have strength to die –

which stresses the winter sterility of nature around them, but also accuses his lover of hypocrisy – why should she be smiling given the state of their relationship? Is it for form's sake or to try and keep up the pretence that they still mean something to each other? But then his lover makes 'a grin of bitterness' which is compared to 'an ominous bird-a-wing'. Some readers of Hardy have made the point that in his poems he uses birds in an ominous and usually pessimistic way – which is only interesting because it contrasts so sharply with the Romantic poets' use of birds in their poems. The Romantics (who preceded Hardy) almost always use birds as symbols of hope, poetic inspiration or the uplifting power of nature. Hardy – it could be argued – is more modern in his sensibility using birds as symbols of something negative and life-denying.

Hardy in the final stanza is writing from an imagined present and writes:

Since then, keen lessons that love deceives,

And wrings with wrong, have shaped to me

Your face, and the God-curst sun, and a tree

And a pond edged with grayish leaves.

'Since then' suggests the incident is long ago. Hardy suggests that he has been in love since then, but without success: he has learnt 'keen lessons' that 'love deceives', and whenever he does his mind thinks back to this unsuccessful meeting by the pond. The alliteration of 'wrings with wrong' sounds unpleasant and the venom (partly in the sound, partly in the meaning) of 'God-curst sun' is very bleak and powerful. In artistic terms Hardy brings the poem full circle to end where he began – the pond, the tree, the gray leaves. The pond is stagnant like the relationship, and is part of the pathetic fallacy used through the poem – the dead leaves, the white sun. The landscape is drained of all colour – just as the relationship is drained of all love.

Byron's 'When We Two Parted' is clearly about one individual woman. Hardy's poem is based on a meeting with one individual woman, but he has learnt 'keen lessons that love deceives' since then, which suggests a series of unsuccessful relationships, with the one in 'Neutral Tones' being the first of many. And in what ways can love deceive? Our first thought might be infidelity, but that is not very subtle. Hardy might mean pretending to yourself that you love someone or falling in love with someone before discovering what they are really like or just falling in love with the wrong person. I'm sure you can think of other possibilities. Hardy is claiming that at the end of any relationship he thinks back to this scene by the pond because of its sterile desolation: perhaps it was also the end of his first serious love affair.

Hardy chooses to use a regular rhyme scheme and the poem is made up of four rhyming quatrains written in iambic tetrameter – eight syllables to the line with four stressed syllables. However, Hardy uses enjambment skillfully and there is some metrical variation: 'God-curst sun' consists of three stressed syllables which adds force and power to the words themselves.

In 'Neutral Tones' Hardy

- writes a devastatingly bleak poem about the end of a relationship;

- uses pathetic fallacy in a masterly way to convey the human emotions in the poem;

- writes with a sense of experience about the bitter feelings that relationships can cause;

- apportions no blame for the breakdown of the relationship;

- uses imagery well to convey the sterility of the landscape and by extension the sterility of the relationship.

'The Farmer's Bride' – Charlotte Mew

Context

Charlotte Mew was born in London in 1869. Her father died in 1898, leaving his family in poverty. Three of her siblings died in childhood and another two suffered from mental illness and were put in hospital permanently. Charlotte and her remaining sister, Anne, made a pact never to marry for fear of passing on insanity to their children. She started publishing short stories in 1896, but her first collection of poetry (for which this poem provided the title) was not published until 1916. After the death of Anne, she descended into a deep depression and eventually committed suicide in 1928.

maid – young girl – the implication is also that she is a virgin

bide – wait

woo – a slightly old-fashioned word now, it means to court or win the affections of someone.

fay – a fairy.

fall – autumn. We associate this word with American English, but there is evidence that it survived as a term for *autumn* in some regions of the UK until at least 1900.

abed – in bed

fast – tightly locked

beseech – to ask or pray earnestly.

leveret – a young hare; more technically, a hare that is less than a year old.

betwixt – between.

Who? The poet speaks as a farmer who has married a young girl who is scared of men and sex. He tells us a lot about his wife. He also has neighbours who help catch his wife when she runs off.

When? The farmer speaks in the past tense before switching to the present in the third stanza.

Where? It is set in a rural community on a farm and there is a closeness to the natural world and the rhythms and seasons of nature expressed through the imagery.

What? The farmer describes what has happened in his life since he got married just over a year before the poem starts.

Commentary

This poem's narrator is a farmer who tells the story of his courtship of his wife and the progress of their three year marriage.

In the first stanza we are told that on reflection he thinks that perhaps she was too young. He married her quickly in the summer of one year because it was harvest time and he had more pressing things to attend to – bringing in the harvest. The marriage has not gone well. We are not told exactly why, but husband and wife do not sleep together and the final line of the opening stanza tells us that the wife tried to run away, because she was so repulsed by her husband and, it is suggested, having sex with her husband. As soon as they were married we are told

... she turned afraid

Of love and me and all things human.

And then *her smile went out* and one night in the autumn she simply ran away.

In the second stanza the husband recounts how he and others from the community chased her in the dark, found her, brought her home and locked her up. She was among the sheep, he was told, but she wasn't and so *we chased her*. It is not clear who *we* are – the farmer and his friends or his neighbours or other members of the community perhaps; what is important, I think, is that it was a group of people chasing after one frightened young woman. They finally caught up with her at Church-town. She was

All in a shiver and a scare

but they ignore her fear, take her home and lock her in the farmer's house. Line 13 is an interesting line. The farmer says she should have been in bed:

Lying awake with her wide brown stare.

We go to bed to sleep, but this line suggests that normally she does not sleep: this suggests that she deliberately stays awake in order not to be taken sexually in her sleep.

In the third stanza the tense changes to describe the present state of affairs. She performs the work about the house and is happy in the company of small creatures

With birds and rabbits and such as they,

but she becomes disturbed whenever any man comes near her. She doesn't say anything but the eyes beseech them not to come near her. The women around the farm have noticed that she seems to have an especial affinity with animals when she speaks to them. The farmer ruefully comments in the final line of the stanza that

I've never heard her speak at all.

The speaker changes tone in the fifth stanza which runs from line 30 to line 41. The first four lines describe his wife in a sympathetic way and in a series of similes all drawn from nature. The sibilance creates a wistful sense of longing - the narrator is clearly attracted to his wife. Line 34 switches to describe the autumn in loving yet elegiac tones: the year is ending, the days are getting shorter, the leaves are falling – there is a sense of nature dying off, all the more beautiful because Mew uses almost wholly monosyllabic words for the rest of the stanza. But in line 39 the narrator mentions the berries on the holly trees getting redder and this reminds him that it will soon be Christmas. The red berries have a symbolic function: red is associated with passion: when a woman's virginity is taken and her hymen broken she often sheds blood: here though the symbol is ironic because sex has not occurred between the farmer and his bride. The stanza ends with the farmer wishing that he had children so that Christmas would be more fulfilling.

What's Christmas-time without there be

Some other in the house than we!

It is one of the central ironies of this poem that farmers produce food which keeps us alive, but this farmer cannot produce children because his wife will not sleep with him.

In the final stanza the voice of the farmer breaks down and, to reflect this, the pattern of the stanza changes and is much shorter and, therefore, more intense. The farmer seems wracked with sexual frustration. His wife sleeps on the floor above him in the attic. So she is physically quite close to him, but not in the same bed. He could reach her very easily, but knows he would frighten her and that she does not want him. Are we to imagine that the attic door is locked? I think we are – or she would run away as she has done before. As he thinks of her he is overwhelmed with physical desire for her youthful skin and the beauty of her eyes and hair. The final sentence begins with an exclamation and then becomes very repetitive as the farmer expresses his almost uncontrolled longing for her. The repetition and the internal rhyme here accentuate his torment and the unfulfilled passion for her:

... Oh! My God! The down,

The soft young down of her, the brown,

The brown of her – her eyes, her hair, her hair!

Down is an interesting word to use because it means and is associated with animals. Throughout the poem the wife has been associated with nature or with things that are not human: *fay, like a hare, like a mouse, a leveret, a young larch tree, the first wild violets.* Furthermore, she has an affinity with animals. Farmers control nature, but the wife is compared or associated with things that we cannot control.

Mew is very successful in creating the voice of the farmer. The vocabulary she uses is very simple and the imagery is drawn from the natural world – the world which the farmer would know so well. There are phrases which suggest a man of little formal education and a slightly old-fashioned or ungrammatical way of expressing himself all through the poem, such as *more's to do, the shut of a winter's day, 'twasn't a woman, runned, her be, fetched her home, men-folk, betwixt.* It is a remarkable feat of ventriloquism. Like other dramatic monologues the speaker reveals more and more of himself as the poem proceeds.

This poem could be read as a simple story of male oppression. After all, the wife tries to run away and now cannot because she is locked in the attic. Her imprisonment here recalls the fate of other fictional heroines such as Mr Rochester's wife in *Jane Eyre* and the central character in *The Yellow Wallpaper* by Charlotte Perkins Gilman. Her association with animals and other natural things might suggest that the farmer is trying to control something natural and force it to do his will; but this imagery is paradoxically the very reason why he finds her so attractive – because she reminds him of the animals he is surrounded by in nature.

However, Mew presents the farmer as essentially sympathetic. He uses his power over her, but he controls his sexual desire for his wife and recognizes that she does not want him. Marital rape was not recognized as a crime in the UK until 1991. In the period that Mew was writing in, it would have been considered normal for the husband to have forced himself onto his wife – it would certainly not have been illegal. But the farmer is perceptive enough to know that she fears him and a sexual relationship. And, although he locks her up, he is, in the context of the times, in control of his urges and sympathetic to her lack of desire for him. His descriptions of her – especially those which compare her to small animals – could be said to display a certain amount of patience towards her – even sympathy or empathy. Equally you could say that these descriptions are slightly condescending and patronizing, because they do not individualize her or see her humanity. We are never told her name and the title of the poem could be said to sum her up: from the farmer's point of view, her only role in life is to be his bride and give him sex and children.

He is not especially cruel to her, but he is rather conventional. He has married in order to have children, perhaps so that they can inherit the farm. He expects her to have sex with him and is filled with frustration that she does not want to. She seems to like animals because, you could argue, she is treated like one: the beasts are kept in their stalls; she is kept in her attic. In addition, we might note that she has a natural affinity which the women have noticed, with small frightened creatures like herself.

Why?

This dramatic monologue

- presents two people trapped in a marriage;

- the wife is literally held prisoner in her husband's house;

- the husband is full of desire for his wife, but sensitive enough to ignore his physical desires;

- examines the imprisoning role that women had to fulfill in the past;

- describes nature in beautiful colloquial language especially in lines 34 to 39;

- shows two people who are both in different ways in tune with nature;

- is full of the wife's fear and the husband's unrequited desires – which can never be reconciled.

'Walking Away' – C Day Lewis

Context

This poem was first published in 1962 in the collection 'The Gate and Other Poems'. It is dedicated to Day-Lewis's first son, Sean, and recalls a day when he was watching Sean go into school. It has become one of his most enduring works and in 2001 was chosen by readers of the *Radio Times* as one of their top ten poems of childhood.

leaves just turning – it is the start of Autumn and the leaves are just turning colour from green to brown and red.

like a satellite – when the poem was written space exploration was in its infancy and satellites were very new, modern things.

pathos – the quality that produces pity.

half-fledged – a fully fledged bird is able to fly, so it follows that Day Lewis's son is not yet capable of independent flight.

gait – manner of walking.

a winged seed – sycamore trees have winged seeds.

irresolute – weak in purpose.

clay – the human body; it has acquired this meaning because in the Christian Bible God makes man from clay.

selfhood – a sense of oneself as a unique individual.

Who? The poet is the speaker of the poem. He is watching his son walk away from him at the end of his first football match, surrounded by the other players. The poem is addressed to his son.

When? The poem was first published in 1962, but is about a memory from 18 years before.

Where? On a school playing field.

What? The poem deals with the son growing up and leaving his close parental bond behind him as he sets out to live his own life. At the end of the poem the tone is one of sadness at this inevitable process and an acceptance too that one's children, one day, have to walk away to their own lives.

Commentary

The first stanza is full of one particular memory. Day Lewis remembers that it is eighteen years since he watched his son play his first football match. The experience has been powerful enough to stay with him and the details – 'the leaves just turning', 'a sunny day' and 'the touch-lines new ruled' – give the memory its vivid quality as does the poet's use of the present tense. At the end of the game Day Lewis watches his son

like a satellite

Wrenched from its orbit, go drifting away...

The word 'away' occurs somewhere in each stanza and three times at the end of a line, emphasizing his son's movement away from him as he grows older. He watches his son walk away from him towards the school

With the pathos of a half-fledged thing set free

Into a wilderness, the gait of one

Who finds no path where the path should be.

He obviously feels his son is not ready for complete freedom yet even though he has started on that path. His plight causes the poet to feel pathos for his son who has been set free but has no path to follow.

This sense of aimless, uninformed movement informs the simile at the opening of the third stanza: his son is a 'hesitant figure' – 'like a winged seed loosed from its parent stem'. This leads Day Lewis to admit that he never manages (either in life or in writing perhaps) to convey

About nature's give and take – the small, the scorching

Ordeals which fire one's irresolute clay.

This looks tricky to understand, but is not really. Nature gives and takes – he is given a son but the son will leave and have an independent life. This causes pain – 'the small, scorching ordeals' – even the tiny ordeal of watching his son walk away from him at the end of a football match. 'Clay' is being used here to mean our personality; however, clay is also used to make vases and plates and it is fixed in position by being 'fired' – heated at very strong temperatures. And so our personalities are fired (created) by our experiences. Watching his son walk away from him causes Day Lewis pain and is a 'small, scorching ordeal' – perhaps one of innumerable ones that Day Lewis feels but which add to his personality.

Despite the football match being eighteen years ago. Day Lewis is haunted by it still:

I have had worse partings, but none that so

Gnaws at my mind still.

Day Lewis suggests tentatively ('perhaps') the sadness he feels at watching his son walk away shows

How selfhood begins with a walking away,

And love is proved in the letting go.

In other words, his son must 'walk away' to become a fully-grown, independent adult and that, because that process is inevitable, true parental love will let go of the child and encourage the child on the road to selfhood.

The readers of the *Radio Times* may have voted this their favourite poem of childhood, but I feel it reveals more about the adult poet and his sadness and regret that his son must 'walk away' and grow up. A parent's natural desire to protect their children from the world and to preserve their innocence is doomed to failure, and the poem is more about Day Lewis's feelings than his son's. The poet's mention of the 'small, scorching ordeals' of everyday life suggest he is sensitive and aware of how the tiniest actions or events in life can trigger strong emotions. This is a poem about how adults cope with seeing their children grow up.

The poem is written in four stanzas of five lines each with the first, the third and the fifth lines rhyming, which suggests that the poet has his feelings under control after years of reflection on the incident. However, only three of the lines are end-stopped and the enjambment suggests the continued strength and distress of his feelings. He feels great pain for what he sees as his son's vulnerability, and the fact that as a parent he can do nothing to stop a process that is inevitable for all children. The final line of the poem brings closure to the angst that the poet feels: 'love is proved in the letting go'.

Overall, despite the hard-won stoicism of the last line, the poem is generally sad and regretful. Its popularity may be due to its relative simplicity – the son's simple act of walking off a football pitch with the other players becoming symbolic of something much larger and universal in its scope. The two similes – the satellite and the spinning tree seed – are easy to relate to, and any reader who has children will identify with the basic premise of the poem – that it is hard to let go of one's children.

In C Day Lewis's 'Walking Away':

- the poet writes movingly about the ordeal and pain that every parent feels as their children grow up;

- comes to an acceptance – memorably expressed in the final line - that the process of growing up is inevitable and that a parent's true love is shown by letting go;

- uses a regular stanza and rhyme scheme but lots of enjambment to show the strength of his feelings;

- uses straightforward language and simple similes to communicate deep and personal feelings.

'Letters from Yorkshire' – Maura Dooley

Context

Maura Dooley was born in Truro, grew up in Bristol, and, after working for some years in Yorkshire, now lives in London. She is a freelance writer and lectures at Goldsmiths' College. She edited *Making for Planet Alice: New Women Poets* (1997) and *The Honey Gatherers: A Book of Love Poems* (2002) for Bloodaxe, and *How Novelists Work* (2000) for Seren. *Life Under Water* (Bloodaxe Books, 2008) is her first new collection since *Sound Barrier: Poems 1982-2002* (Bloodaxe Books, 2002), since then her others include *Explaining Magnetism* (1991) and *Kissing a Bone* (1996), both Poetry Book Society Recommendations. *Kissing a Bone* was shortlisted for the T.S. Eliot Prize and *Life Under Water* has been shortlisted for the T. S. Eliot Prize 2008. This poem was first published in 2002 in a collection called *Sound Barrier*.

Who? The poet writes as herself and about an unidentified 'you' who lives in Yorkshire and is male. The first stanza begins with third person narration, but swiftly changes to direct address of 'you'. By the final stanza Dooley is using the third person plural – 'our'.

When? The poem was published in 2002 in a collection called *Sound Barrier*. It has a contemporary setting.

Where? The poem is addressed to someone living in Yorkshire, while the poet lives in the city (presumably London).

What? The poem juxtaposes the two very different life styles that the poet and the person living in Yorkshire lead, but celebrates the fact that they keep in touch.

Commentary

This poem is about a long-distance relationship conducted by letters – quite an old-fashioned form of communication in the early 21st century. The speaker of the poem lives and works in London (or another big city) as a journalist; the other person lives in Yorkshire in a rural environment and the poem presents these two contrasting lifestyles very vividly. The relationship is one of simple friendship: the speaker asserts in the second stanza – 'It's not romance', simply friendship. In fact, the nature of the relationship is never made clear: the poet is female and appears to be talking as herself, while her friend is male but clearly not a relative.

The first stanza uses the third person – he' – and the past tense. Dooley uses the stanza to introduce the rural setting that the letter writer inhabits and the fact that he writes to her about nature and the chores he does outside:

In February, digging the garden, planting his potatoes,

he saw the first lapwings return and came indoors

to write to me....

Here the present participles 'digging' and 'planting' suggest that these are two activities he is constantly engaged in or engaged in every February, and there is the strong implication that he is going to write to her about what he has just been doing and the return of the lapwings after their winter migration. Dooley has enough empathy or knows enough about his lifestyle to imagine 'his knuckles singing/as they reddened in the warmth'.

Line 5 is succinct and emphatic and marks a change to the present tense: 'It's not romance, just the way things are.' Dooley then makes clear that the real subject of the poem is the contrast in their lifestyles and she switches to the second person:

You out there, in the cold, seeing the seasons

turning, me with my headful of headlines,

feeding words onto a blank screen.

The alliteration of 'headful of headlines' draws attention to itself and underlines one difference in their life styles: headlines change every day, but watching the seasons turn is a slower, more relaxed activity. He grows potatoes which are eaten; she feeds 'words onto a blank screen'. At the end of the third stanza Dooley asks: 'Is your life more real because you dig and sow?'

In the fourth stanza Dooley states the 'you wouldn't say so' - that he would not agree that his life is more real than hers. However, in the same sentence she includes two very 'real' things that he does which strongly suggests that she thinks his life is more real. The whole quotation reads:

You wouldn't say so, breaking ice on a waterbutt,

clearing a path through the snow.

Once again we notice the present participles – 'breaking', 'clearing' – which suggest these are regular activities, and they are activities which are more physically real than a 'headful of headlines'. There is a tone of gratitude in the next lines which suggest that Dooley feels unhappy in the city and craves the realities of life in the countryside and the realities of the natural world:

it's you

who sends me of that other world

pouring light and air into an envelope.

The last line in this quotation is a metaphor and a very fresh and beautiful one: we all need light and air to see and to breathe – and her friend's letters from Yorkshire perform a vital function in her life. They remind her of the real world of nature, the seasons and physical work – things that she is sheltered from in the city. Dooley claims earlier 'It's not romance' (referring to the relationship), but she seems to regard life in the countryside as romantic and it provides her with 'light and air' in the sterile environment of the city.

The end of the poem shows their close connection to each other:

at night, watching the same news in different houses,

our souls tap out messages across the icy miles.

'Our souls' – right at the end of the poem Dooley switches to the first person plural to show their closeness and familiarity with one another. It has been suggested that tapping out messages is a reference to Morse code or even to texting, but it is their souls that are sending the messages. Texting is just too banal and mundane – the point surely is that they are so in tune with one another that their souls communicate 'across the icy miles' – the poem ending with a memorable piece of assonance.

Dooley contrasts the two lifestyles very effectively in this poem and in such a way that she makes clear she reveres and misses the real, outdoor life in Yorkshire. Her friends letters are filled with details of what he is doing on the land and the arrival of wildlife – his letters are her source of 'air and light' – which suggests that she finds her current lifestyle suffocating and stultifying. Her job as a journalist deals with news that changes every day; his work in Yorkshire involves repeated actions – he probably plants potatoes every February – but his activities are more in tune with nature and the rhythms of the seasons.

For the most part Dooley uses every-day, straightforward language and little figurative language. She uses quite long sentences and lots of enjambment, so that when she does write a short sentence it stands out and is foregrounded – as she does in lines 5 and 9.

Interestingly the poem raises the question of news. The poet with her 'head full of headlines' works as a newspaper journalist. This is contrasted with the 'news' of the lapwings' arrival after their winter absence and the news that her friend had to break the ice on the water butt. The poem questions what we classify as 'news' – the daily-changing diet of headlines we are fed or the age-old rituals of gardening and farming. Of course, we need and value both, but only one provides us with 'air and light'.

The issue of communication is an important one in the poem. We have already noted that the hand-written personal letters that the poet's friend sends her are old-fashioned in today's world of texts and emails and WhatApp, but it takes more time to write a personal letter, to address it and to take it to the post box to post it – more evidence that the lifestyle of the man is slower and allows him more time and that he takes the time and trouble to write the letters. The poet is a journalist but communicates with headlines – which in the era of online news and news feeds are subject to almost continual change. Finally, in the final line, we reach the poem's climax in which their souls are said to communicate with each other despite their geographical separateness.

'Letters from Yorkshire' by Maura Dooley:

- deals with a platonic, non-romantic relationship between the poet and a man who lives in Yorkshire;

- contrasts her sterile urban existence and her job with the natural rhythms of life and his work in the countryside (which Dooley presents as more real and satisfying);

- poses the question of what we classify and value as 'news';

- explores different ways of communicating.

'Eden Rock' – Charles Causley

Context

Charles Stanley Causley, CBE, FRSL (24 August 1917 – 4 November 2003) was a Cornish poet, schoolmaster and writer. His work is noted for its simplicity and directness and for its associations with folklore, especially when linked to his native Cornwall. At a time when poetry was becoming experimental and often very esoteric, Causley persisted with traditional forms (as he does in this poem), and breathed fresh life into them.

somewhere beyond – a suitably vague location.

a sprigged dress – embroidered with representations of twigs.

a screw of paper – a scrunched wad of paper which acts as a cork.

from the other bank – his parents are the other side of the stream, but, as we shall see, this phrase has deeper connotations.

Who? Charles Causley and his parents.

When? The poem is written in the present tense, but Causley appears to be looking back with affectionate nostalgia on past events.

Where? Eden Rock – a picturesque location that Causley invented for the sake of the poem. The choice of 'Eden' suggests paradise and this links with the intense nostalgia in most of the poem.

What? In the poem his parents are having a picnic and inviting him to cross a stream to join them.

Commentary

Most readers treat this poem as a simple exercise in nostalgia and an expression of love and affection for his parents. Certainly on one level, the poem works like this, but (as we shall see) there are other elements in the poem which work to make it more than a simple nostalgia narrative.

In the first stanza Causley's parents are waiting for him 'Somewhere beyond Eden Rock' – a suitably mysterious location. The first two stanzas establish that his parents are relatively young too and even his father's dog is 'still two years old'. His mother lays a table cloth over the grass and pours tea from a Thermos. There is the affectionate memory of trivial details which give a sense of verisimilitude: the milk 'in an old H.P. Sauce bottle' and 'the same three plates, the tin cups painted blue'. His father wears the 'same suit', but the same suit as what? The same suit that Causley remembers seeing him in often?

This is presented as a familiar scene from Causley's childhood, and he uses the present tense to give it immediacy and vibrancy, but it seems as if he is writing about a time before he was born. He is physically separated from his parents and before his mother looks at him, 'The sky whitens as if lit by three suns' – a strange and momentous image.

In the final stanza his parents call to him:

They beckon to me from the other bank,

I hear them call, 'See where the stream path is!

Crossing is not as hard as you might think.'

Before we consider the final line, we should consider the form of the poem. Causley writes in regular quatrains, but uses different types of half-rhyme at the end of every line – in fact, he only uses full rhyme at the end with 'this' and 'is'. Half-rhyme is often used by poets when they want to suggest something is wrong.

And certainly something is wrong. After all the nostalgic images, Causley's clear affection for his parents and the idyllic surroundings, the last line introduces a sinister note of unease which is foregrounded by the line being not physically part of the final stanza – the line's isolation suggesting the poet's isolation or sense of isolation:

I did not think it would be like this.

This line is vague, but it is totally at odds with the cheery optimism of the rest of the poem and suggests that 'it', life, has been very different from what Causley expected – it has not been one long picnic in the moors 'somewhere beyond Eden Rock'. His parents did not stay twenty-five and twenty-three forever. Indeed, it is quite possible that Causley wrote this poem after their deaths – the underworld is separated from the land of the living by a stream as Causley is in the poem. Thinking about the title it is worth remembering that, although the Garden of Eden was Paradise, Adam and Eve were ejected from Eden. The image of the sky whitening as if 'lit by three suns' inevitably suggests the atomic bombs that were dropped on Hiroshima and Nagasaki.

In the poem Causley's parents are frozen in a time before he was born, having a picnic and waiting for him to join them in life – a life in which they will go on similar picnics – but not for long. Causley was born in 1917 and his father, who fought in the First World War, died of his wounds when Causley was only seven – a devastating loss for one so young. If Causley's father died when he was seven, there cannot have been many family picnics like the one described in the poem. Perhaps the scene that Causley describes is imaginary – one he wishes he had had, but did not because of his father's early death. During the Second World War Causley served in the Royal Navy – an experience that affected him profoundly and as a writer in the 1950s and 1960s he was well aware of the threat of nuclear weapons.

Therefore, what appears as a nostalgic tribute to his parents, is really an elegy to them and to all the horrors of life in the twentieth century. As Causley puts it in stunningly simple English:

I did not think it would be like this.

As readers we realize that the idyllic picnic beyond Eden Rock probably never happened except in Causley's imagination – which adds to the sense of devastation and loss at the end of the poem.

An alternative reading might be that Causley's parents are dead, frozen in the ages at which he remembers them, and that they are calling to him from beyond the grave in a picnic scene that Causley remembers. We are still left with the unsettling and devastating last line – 'I did not think it would be like this', in which the simple monosyllabic words, completely devoid of any figurative language – spell out a harsh and threatening truth. What does Causley mean by 'it'? The answer is surely simple – life, human existence, the world as it is.

In 'Eden Rock' Charles Causley

- uses a simple form to write what appears to be a poem of nostalgia about childhood;

- writes not a tribute to his parents or to his childhood, but an elegy to them and the lost innocence of his childhood world;

- in his devastating last line combines the deeply personal with the wider implications of being alive in the 20th century;

- uses the simile 'as if lit by three suns' to move the poem to a higher level and to ensure the poem moves beyond family picnics – which probably never happened as described in the poem.

'Follower' – Seamus Heaney

Context

Seamus Heaney was born on 13 April 1939 and died on 30 August 2013. Heaney was an Irish poet, widely recognized as one of the best poets writing in English in the late 20th and early 21st centuries. He was awarded the Nobel Prize for Literature in 1995. He was born and brought up in Northern Ireland, but lived in the Republic of Ireland from 1973. Heaney considered himself an Irish poet and objected to being included in collections of 'British' poets. Northern Ireland has had a violent and troubled history, but Heaney's poems (even those which do address political concerns) are always deeply personal and rooted in everyday events and circumstances. This poem (first published in 1966 in the collection *Death of a Naturalist*) explores his relationship with his father – as do several other poems in that collection.

the shafts – the two parallel wooden handles that the ploughman uses to control the direction of the plough.

the furrow – the trench made by a plough.

the wing – the stabilizers on either side of the plough.

sock – the ploughshare – the sharpened metal that cuts through the soil.

headrig – a headland in a ploughed field.

the sweating team – the team of two horses pulling the plough.

the polished sod – the earth upturned by the plough; it is polished because it is damp.

Who? The speaker in the poem is Heaney himself, writing about his father.

When? Most of the poem is set in Heaney's childhood, in the past, but the final sentence brings us sharply back to the present.

Where? In a generalized rural setting.

What? Heaney describes his father's skill and prowess as a ploughman, and the way he idolized him, but in a poignant ending notes that their positions are now reversed. The title, we realize by the end of the poem, is deliberately ambiguous.

Commentary

'Follower' is a well-known poem by Seamus Heaney and it has often been studied at GCSE. There is a reason for that: it is a very good poem and, at its end, very poignant and moving. Heaney was born into a farming family and a large part of the poem is a eulogy or tribute to his father's skill as a ploughman – the way he controlled the horses which pulled the plough, the way he controlled the plough as it cut a furrow in an un-ploughed field, and his general expertise as a ploughman. The poem ends rather unexpectedly with a reflection on old age and the relationship between father and son.

The poem is divided into 6 four-line stanzas and has a strict rhyme scheme, although Heaney occasionally uses half-rhyme instead of full rhyme. This regularity mimics the precision of the ploughing process which we know has to be precise and at which Heaney's father is 'an expert'. Keeping to a pattern also recalls the fields full of straight furrows after they have been ploughed. The regular rhythm also mimics the movement of the horses pulling the plough and Heaney's father's footsteps plodding behind them.

The poem starts with a simple statement: 'My father worked with a horse-plough' – as in the photo above. 'His shoulders globed like a full sail' contains a simile ('like a full sail') which suggests something large and expansive, but 'globed' is a metaphor which suggests the size and strength of Heaney's father's back, but also suggests his father's importance to him: he is his whole world (globe). His father controls the horses with his 'clicking tongue'. Heaney's understanding of the technical terms to do with ploughing and the parts of the plough – 'shafts', 'furrow', 'wing', 'sock', 'headrig' – suggests the younger Heaney's interest in ploughing.

The second stanza opens with a two word sentence which is foregrounded by being only two words long, but also at the start of the stanza – isolated and drawing attention to itself. The stanza focuses on what Heaney's father does – setting the wing and fitting the sock. Everything is presented in a positive way, even the sod 'rolled over without breaking' and when they reach the end of the field Heaney's father uses 'a single pluck' to make the horses turn around to plough the next furrow.

Not only does Heaney's father possess complete and expert control of the plough and the horses, he also possesses a good eye which

Narrowed and angled at the ground,

Mapping the furrow exactly.

Stanza four concentrates on Heaney as a boy. He sometimes stumbled in his father's 'hob-nailed wake' or fell on the 'polished sod': so, in contrast to his father who is an expert, Heaney is a clumsy child.

The fifth stanza conveys a sense of regret. As a young boy, all Heaney wanted to do was to be an expert ploughman like his father: 'to close one eye, stiffen my arm'. He revered and idolized his father so much:

All I ever did was follow

His broad shadow round the farm.

The sixth and final stanza sees Heaney looking back at his childhood and he admits

I was a nuisance, tripping, falling,

Yapping always.

The final sentence is crucial to the impact of the poem and deserves a lot of attention. Note how it switches to the present tense:

But today

It is my father who keeps stumbling

Behind me, and will not go away.

Now their roles are reversed and the title of the poem – 'Follower' could easily refer to both father and son. As parents age they become more dependent on their adult children, and now it is Heaney's father who is a nuisance and will not go away. The followed has become the follower. I think Heaney still respects the good, honest toil and the skill in ploughing, but he has chosen a different path in life – university and the life of a writer. In that sense he has not followed his father in the life of a farmer, as he thought he would as a young boy.

And so what began as a eulogy to Heaney's father and to Heaney's own childhood ambitions becomes a lament on the dependency of old age and the inevitable reversal of roles that occurs between father and son as the father ages. As a result the tone of the poem changes radically. What appeared to be a nostalgic poem about childhood, full of adoration and reverence for his father is transformed by the last sentence into a lament about the inevitable reversal of roles that old age can bring.

'Follower' by Seamus Heaney:

- evokes a strong sense of the skill and physical force required to be a good ploughman;

- successfully presents the reverence and admiration that most young boys feel towards their father;

- shows how childhood ambitions can change;

- demonstrates a detailed knowledge of the technicalities of ploughing;

- in the poignant final sentence shows how the father and son relationship can be reversed.

'Mother, any distance' Simon Armitage

Context

Simon Armitage was born in 1963 in the village of Marsden in West Yorkshire and has spent most of his life in that area. He is a very successful and highly-regarded poet, celebrated for his down-to-earth language and subject matter. His poetry often (but not always) deals with the ordinary incidents and events of modern life and appear to be based on personal experience. However, as his career as a poet has progressed, his subject matter has widened impressively.

pelmets – a fringe or other device for hiding a curtain rod.

Who? Armitage addresses the poem to his mother.

When? The setting is contemporary. The poem was first published in 1993.

Where? In Armitage's new house.

What? Armitage's mother is at the house to help in the process of measuring for curtains etc..

Commentary

This is a poem that explores the poet's relationship with his mother in a witty way through the use of an extended metaphor based on the exploration of space. Despite the witty conceit, Armitage raises important questions – to which many readers will be able to relate - towards the end of the poem.

The setting is mundane and domestic. Armitage and his mother are in his new house taking measurements for curtains, carpets and the like – a task which by its very nature requires two people since 'any distance greater than a single span/requires a second pair of hands'. The poet is faced with 'the acres of the walls, the prairies of the floors' – the huge distances implied by the metaphorical 'acres' and 'prairies' perhaps suggesting Armitage's nervousness at moving out of his parents' home into a home of his own: it is an important step in one's growing independence.

In the second stanza his mother is at the zero end while Armitage unreels the spool of the tape measure, calling back to his mother precise measurements in 'metres, centimetres,' 'back to base' – the first phrase which suggests the world of space exploration. The fact that his mother is the 'base' shows how important she still is in the poet's life. The poet writes that the tape measure feeding out is 'unreeling years between us' – the years that separate them but also all the shared experiences of those years. The second quatrain ends in two single word metaphorical sentences. Anchors keep boats moored in one place, and his mother is his anchor because she provides him with stability in stormy weather, difficult times. By contrast, Armitage is a kite, borne aloft by the wind and flying free, but still attached by a line to his mother. The tape measure also represents all the years that Armitage and his mother have shared which also strengthens the familial bond between them.

The sestet begins with Armitage space-walking 'through the empty bedrooms', the tape measure is now metaphorically the line that attaches an astronaut to his spaceship and provides him with oxygen. Armitage makes no explicit reference to it, but the reader cannot help feeling that the tape also represents the umbilical cord that joins a mother to her baby – a connection between mother and child that never ceases to exist.

Armitage climbs the ladder into the loft, while down below his mother's 'fingertips still pinch/the last one hundredth of an inch'. The poet feels he is 'at breaking point, where something has to give'. Then the poem ends

...I reach

towards a hatch that opens on an endless sky

to fall or fly.

The 'endless sky' represents all the possibilities and promises of an adult, independent existence, and, in a show of brave honesty, the poet admits he may fall to earth and metaphorically die or he may fly – live a successful independent existence, while keeping his relationship with his mother intact. 'To fall or fly' is a beautifully succinct way of expressing these alternatives (foregrounded by the alliteration on *f*), and the metaphor of being an astronaut walking in space builds up to the final line.

The poem begins with a regular rhyme scheme in the first quatrain, but this formality breaks down as the poem progresses with irregular line lengths especially in the third verse. In some ways, despite its irregularity, it resembles a sonnet with two quatrains followed by a sestet and an extra, short, fifteenth line. This breaking down of formality on Armitage's part is deliberate: it reflects the growing uncertainty and uneasiness he feels as he gets further and further from his mother and 'base camp'. It is a perfect example of form mirroring content as he moves from a formal, structured opening to an irregular panicky sestet and leaves all rules of formality behind. This mirrors both his continued need for his mother and his nervousness about setting up house on his own. The poem even begins in a verbally formal way with the use of 'Mother' and 'requires'.

Simon Armitage's 'Mother any distance':

- presents the closeness of the mother/child relationship. Armitage may be an adult setting up home on his own, but he still needs his mother;

- uses the tape measure as a shifting symbol – umbilical cord, mountaineering rope and oxygen supply tube when Armitage introduces the idea of an astronaut on a space-walk;

- uses form and its disintegration to suggest the nervousness and disquiet that Armitage feels;

- ends with a potentially frightening image that we all must face when we leave home and start independent lives – 'to fall or fly;

- implies an affectionate tenderness between mother and son, and a reluctance on Armitage's part to let go, while recognizing that he must become an independent adult.

'Before You Were Mine' – Carol Ann Duffy

Context

Carol Ann Duffy is one of the UK's most successful and best-known living poets. Her poems have a very wide appeal. On May 1st 2009 she became the nation's Poet Laureate – the first woman ever to hold the position. Her poems are often set for study by the examination boards – because they are thought of very highly and because many of them are very accessible. Her poems often use very modern and everyday language, but in fresh, funny and witty ways. She uses traditional forms like the sonnet and the dramatic monologue, but succeeds in breathing new life into these old forms by the modernity of her writing and subject matter. The accessibility of many of her poems may obscure the fact that she is highly skilled at a very intricate and ingenious manipulation of language.

Marilyn – a reference to a famous photo of Marilyn Monroe.

the ballroom with a thousand eyes – the mirror ball that hangs down from the centre of the ceiling at dances and discos, although the 'thousand eyes' may be the five hundred pairs of men's eyes looking at the women at the dance and checking them out.

relics – here venerated objects that once belonged to someone revered and famous: Duffy's mother's red shoes.

George Square – a famous and lively square in Glasgow city centre.

Portobello – a famous beach in an eastern suburb of Edinburgh.

Who? Duffy addresses her mother directly in this poem.

When? In the past – Duffy is trying to recreate through words her mother's life before she gave birth to the poet.

Where? Duffy's mother grew up and lived in Glasgow, so most of the poem is set in Glasgow.

What? The poem acts as a homage to her mother's life before she became pregnant along with a recognition of the responsibilities that being a mother brings and the changes to one's lifestyle that being a parent necessitates.

Commentary

'Before You Were Mine' is a joyous and exuberant celebration of the life of Carol Ann Duffy's mother before the poet was born. As such Duffy lovingly tries to recreate the scenes and the atmosphere of those years, before Duffy herself was born.

The poem opens in the present tense ten years before Duffy's birth – 'I'm ten years from the corner you laugh on /with your pals, Maggie McGeeney and Jean Duff'. The use of specific names gives the poem added intimacy and verisimilitude. The three girls are in high spirits on an evening out and 'shriek at the pavement' because they are in such an excited frame of mind. In the last line of the stanza Duffy writes 'Your polka dot dress blows round your legs. Marilyn'. With one word – 'Marilyn' – Duffy evokes the glamourous image of the film star Marilyn Monroe and also refers to an iconic photograph (see above) of her: she is suggesting that her mother was as glamourous in her own way as Marilyn Monroe and shared the same enthusiasm for life.

The second stanza is in the present tense and starts with a simple statement – 'I'm not here yet' – to remind us that Duffy is not alive, although she is writing about her mother's life as if she were. Duffy's mother is so preoccupied with the "ballroom with the thousand eyes, the fizzy, movie tomorrows/the right walk home could bring' that 'the thought of me doesn't occur'. The 'right walk home' is with a good-looking man and it conjures up images of a better and exciting future – the 'fizzy, movie tomorrows' – ending in love and marriage as many movies of the time did. Her mother always gets home late to find her own mother standing 'at the close [the entrance to their flat] with a hiding [a beating] for the late one'. Duffy comments, with a tone of admiration at her mother's rebelliousness and vivacity: 'You figure it's worth it' – worth it for the 'right walk home' with a handsome man.

The third stanza's first line brings the reality of motherhood a little closer:

The decade ahead of my loud, possessive yell was the best one, eh?

The informal 'eh?' at the end of the line establishes mother and daughter's intimacy and the informal closeness that exists between them, as though Duffy's mother has shared many intimate memories of those years with Duffy. In the next sentence Duffy is writing as an adult looking back on her childhood when she used to play with her mother's eye-catching red shoes: 'I remember my hands in those high-heeled red shoes' which are now treated as 'relics' of her mother's youthful days. She then claims to see her mother's ghost, the ghost of her youthful self, 'clear as scent' (the scent she is wearing) coming clattering (on her high heels) towards the poet in George Square. Her mother in the past seems to be fresh from some romantic encounter and the stanza ends with Duffy asking her 'whose small love bites [are] are on your neck, sweetheart?' The use of 'sweetheart' is interesting: on one hand, it is a term of genuine endearment from Duffy to her mother, but on the other it is the word that the men who chase her might well use to address her.

Stanza four starts with an onomatopoeic attempt to render dance steps which Duffy's mother taught her 'on the way home from Mass'. Her mother is said to be 'stamping stars from the wrong pavement' and this metaphor sums up her mother: the stars are glamourous; 'stamping' suggests an inner strength; and 'the wrong pavement' suggests her non-conformity. Even then 'before I was born' Duffy writes, I wanted 'the bold girl winking in Portobello' – bold and winking at men she fancies, we assume. The last sentence of the poem is a brilliant ending to what precedes it:

That glamourous love lasts

Where you sparkle and waltz and laugh before you were mine.

The last words of the poem neatly use the title itself, and Duffy asserts her love for her mother and her love and reverence for her mother's younger self.

The poem is written in a familiar, confidential and informal way with many contractions, single word sentences and interjections from normal speech – 'eh?' The conceit of pretending to know about her life before Duffy was born is witty in itself and the present tense allows the reader to accept this idea. Some readers have suggested that the poem is inspired by old photos of Duffy and her friends; I think the detail comes from anecdotes – things that Duffy's mother has told her with, perhaps, some invented details.

Despite the youthful joy and exuberance that are celebrated in the poem, there is something else going on: Duffy's love for her mother is very possessive as the possessive pronoun – mine – in the title suggests. She also refers to her 'loud, possessive yell' – being a parent brings with it enormous responsibilities. The poem seems to suggest that Duffy is slightly jealous that she did not know her mother when she was younger – she certainly falls in love with the image of her mother from the time before she was born. Duffy uses imagery of colour, smell and light to romanticize her mother's earlier life before she gave birth to her daughter.

In 'Before You Were Mine' Carol Ann Duffy:

- writes a eulogy to her mother's younger self;

- associates her mother with glamourous images of light and of famous actresses;

- writes a joyous poem of youthful sexual exuberance;

- also shows the possessive love that a child can have for its parent and the difficulties of being a mother.

'Winter Swans' – Owen Sheers

Context

Owen Sheers is a Welsh poet, author and scriptwriter. He has published two poetry collections, *The Blue Book* and *Skirrid Hill* which won a Somerset Maugham Award. His debut prose work *The Dust Diaries*, a non-fiction narrative set in Zimbabwe won the Welsh Book of the Year 2005. Owen's first novel, Resistance has been translated into ten languages. Owen co-wrote the screenplay for the film adaptation, released in the UK in 2011. In 2009 he published the novella White Ravens, a contemporary response to the myth of Branwen Daughter of Llyr, as part of Seren's 'New Stories from the Mabinogion series.

Owen's theatrical writing includes his libretto for Rachel Portman's oratorio, *The Water Diviner's Tale*, which premiered at the Royal Albert Hall for the BBC Proms in 2007. *Unicorns*, almost a one man play about the life and work of WWII poet Keith Douglas, was developed with Old Vic, New Voices. In Easter 2011 Owen wrote the script and novelization (*The Gospel of Us*) for *The Passion*, National Theatre of Wales' 72 hour site-specific production in Port Talbot starring and directed by Michael Sheen. The Observer described the production as 'the theatrical event of the decade'. Owen's short play *The Fair & Tender* was performed as part of the Bush Theatre's 66 Books.

tipping – when swans feed they immerse the top half of their bodies – head, bill, neck and all - at 90 degrees to the lower half of their bodies, so that only the bottom half of their body is visible, sticking up out of the water. This known as tipping.

in unison - simultaneously

stilling – in the act of becoming still; an original and striking usage.

Who? The speaker of the poem and his or her lover.

When? The poem was published in 2005 in the collection *Skirrid Hill*.

Where? Unspecified – but near a lake where swans swim.

What? The speaker of the poem reflects on his/her relationship with his or her lover.

Commentary

The first stanza makes it clear that it has been raining incessantly for two days. In a break in the rain the lovers take a walk. Note Sheers' use of alliteration in the final line which highlights the couple's lack of communication. Given what follows in the rest of the poem, it is tempting to see the 'two days of rain' as a pathetic fallacy for the state of their relationship. The 'waterlogged earth' is 'gasping for breath' as if fighting for its very existence in Sheers' personification of it; perhaps their relationship is also 'gasping for breath'. The lovers 'skirted the lake', 'silent and apart'; 'skirted' can mean to go round the edge of something – in this case the lake – but you can also skirt round an issue – perhaps an issue the couple don't want to confront. Certainly the couple are 'silent and apart' – perhaps they have nothing to say to each other or perhaps they know that they will bicker if they try to communicate.

In the third stanza the swans 'came and stopped us' with 'a show of tipping in unison'. Swans are remarkably beautiful and elegant birds, even when engaged in the simple act of feeding. In the UK swans enjoy the protection of the Crown – all unmarked swans belong to the Queen – and as a result they are not hunted. Swans are a part of Western culture, often occurring in fairy tale or myth. The movement of swans tipping is so elegant the speaker wonders (in a simile) whether they are 'rolling weights down their bodies to their heads'. To the onlooker it appears that they have 'halved themselves in the dark water'; in a metaphor they are compared to 'icebergs of white feather' before they re-emerge from the water 'like boats righting in rough weather'. If swans and boats can right themselves (return to an upright position), then perhaps there is a chance that the couple can return to a state of happiness and equilibrium.

As the swans fly off, Sheers allows the speaker's lover to speak: "They mate for life,' you said. Having been compared to icebergs (big and dangerous and white), Sheers uses a much more fragile and beautiful metaphor to describe the swans – they are 'porcelain over the stilling lake'. Porcelain is a fragile but beautiful creation. 'Stilling' is an original and interesting usage: 'stilling' gives the impression that the water is slowly and gradually becoming still.

The speaker does not reply to the point about swans mating for life and they continue to walk around the lake, but whereas before they had skirted the lake they now are now 'slow-stepping' – together and slowly – just as the swans tipped in unison, The last sentence of the poem is long and a real tour-de-force, leading up to the climax in the last line.

The speaker notices that as they have walked slowly along the 'lake's shingle and sand',

...our hands that had somehow,

swum the distance between us,

and folded, one over the other,

like a pair of wings settling after flight

This ending is rich in metaphors and Sheers ensures they are closely related to swans and water. Their hands swim between them to hold each other's hand; the hands fold over one another as a swan's wings fold over one another and the final simile 'like a pair of wings settling after flight' suggests strongly a reconciliation between the two lovers prompted by the sight of the swans and the remark that they mate for life. The lovers' hands settling after flight become one joined set of wings, united and reconciled. After the flight of their disagreements, they have now settled into reconciliation. However, observant readers will notice that Sheers omits the full stop at the end of the final sentence: is this to suggest that not all the couple's problems have been resolved and that they face further 'rainy days' ahead?

This is a poem about reconciliation and the catalysts for the reconciliation are the swans. The swans are beautiful in themselves; their tipping is a graceful motion and the simile Sheers uses to get them upright again – 'like boats righting in rough weather' – demonstrates to the couple that things can be righted. Then comes the observation that swans are monogamous (as are several species of birds). The lovers hands reunite in a metaphor drawn from water – 'they had swum the distance between us' – and the hands folded over remind us of the swans – 'like a pair of wings settling after flight'; the 'flight' in this case being the couple's lack of communication at the start of the poem. The lovers have learnt from the swans, and the sight and grace of the swans have encouraged their reconciliation, although that reconciliation is subdued and delicately tentative –as the missing full stop implies.

The location deserves attention. The poet uses a lake in winter and uses the weather to suggest what has been going on in the relationship. 'The clouds had given their all' – it has rained incessantly for two days and the ground is waterlogged. After the swans depart, the water on the lake is 'stilling' – calm is being restored to the landscape and to the relationship: their walk slows and their hands come together.

The poem is written in free verse with occasional internal rhyme. The first six stanzas all have three lines, but the last poem has two – mirroring the two hands that are now joined together as closely as a swan's wings.

Owen Sheers' 'Winter Swans' is:

- a tender poem which enacts a tentative reconciliation between two lovers;

- uses the swans as both a metaphor and a catalyst for the reconciliation achieved at the end of the poem;

- matches the visual elegance of the swans with a restrained elegance of the words, especially in the beautiful last stanza.

'Singh Song!' – Daljit Nagra

Context

Daljit Nagra was born in 1966 to Punjabi Indian parents. He has been hailed as one of the most exciting poets of his generation. His first collection *Look We Have Coming to Dover!* is full of monologues which attempt to capture the experience in Britain of the Indian working classes. His poetry is preoccupied with what it is like to be an Asian growing up and living in Britain, so his work touches on issues of belonging, identity, racism, but also what it means to be British. It is a stereotype of Indian-ness that they run corner shops; when many Indians first arrived in the UK, it was certainly one quick and legitimate way for them to establish themselves in business, because they could buy a corner shop and run it as they chose without any barriers because of their race.

he vunt me – he wants me.

chapatti – unleavened Indian bread.

chutney – another staple of Indian cuisine. A side dish made from fruit or vegetables and designed to be eaten with bread or poppadoms.

Putney – apart from being an area of South West London, 'putney' is also the Punjabi word for 'wife'. Putney is on the Thames and lots of rowing clubs practise there. Every year the river at Putney hosts the Oxford and Cambridge Boat Race.

effing – swearing profusely.

di tickle of my bride – a euphemism for sex.

di brighty moon – clearly this means the moon is bright, but there may be a play on words. 'Brighty' is very similar to the word 'Blighty' which British people used to use as a word signifying Great Britain. 'Blighty' itself is the Hindi word for 'home'.

Who? The narrator is Singh, an Indian shopkeeper who runs one of his father's shops. There are references to his parents, to his new bride and to the customers of his shop. The poem is a dramatic monologue because the poet adopts a voice which is clearly not his own.

When? Now – in the early 21st century. The poem describes a typical day for the narrator and ends in the evening when the moon is visible.

Where? In the narrator's father's shop and the flat upstairs where his new bride waits for him. The mention of Putney in line 9 suggests it might be set in south west London, but the word 'putney' has other connotations. It is the Punjabi word for wife and, bearing in mind the strenuous activity involved in rowing, the simile 'like we rowing through Putney' is very sexual in its connotations and suggests very strenuous sex.

What? Singh describes his day in the shop and the time he spends with his wife upstairs in the flat. Apart from two italicized interjections by the dissatisfied voices of his customers, this is a dramatic monologue as Nagra adopts a voice that is not his.

Commentary

In this amusing yet ultimately tender poem, Nagra adopts the voice of a young Indian man in the UK who runs one of his father's corner shops. This partly corresponds to a racial stereotype about Indians running corner shops in urban or suburban areas. Nagra embraces the stereotype and reveals a truth behind the image. Although the overall effect is deeply funny, the poem also raises serious questions about identity and culture.

The title of the poem is a pun. The narrator is a Sikh and Singh is a common Sikh name; in addition, many people say that Indians speak English in a sing-song manner because of the rhythm in which they speak English. So it is the song of Singh and it also reflects the way he speaks: throughout the poem Nagra uses phonetic spelling to imitate Singh's accent and his use of half-rhyme and full rhyme increase the poem's song-like qualities as do the two italicized verses where Singh's customers speak, providing a sort of chorus to the main part of the poem which is Singh's description of his life.

The opening two stanzas tell us about the narrator's situation: he runs one of his father's shops and is expected to be open from nine in the morning until nine at night. But when there are no customers Singh shuts the shop and goes upstairs to make love to his wife. He prioritizes love over business. In the poem he and his wife reject the traditional values of business which his father and mother's generation hold so dear. Singh tells us that 'from 9 o'clock to 9 o'clock/and he [his father] vunt me not to have a break', but he takes frequent breaks to go upstairs to make love to his wife. The stereotype that Nagra is subverting is that of the well-run Indian corner shop, managed by someone in the family, and open and accessible at all hours.

The third stanza describes what happens when he returns downstairs to the shop. The lines in italics are the voices of his customers who pour out a litany of complaints about his shop, concluding that Singh's is

... *di worst Indian shop*

on di whole Indian road.

The next three stanzas are devoted to his new wife and we can see that he is totally obsessed with her. Each stanza begins *my bride* – which suggests they have not been married for very long. He hears her high heels tapping above his head and imagines her flirting with other men on a Sikh dating website. He seems to get vicarious pleasure from this – knowing that other men find her attractive. There is a funny play on words: Singh's wife

...is playing wid mouse

ven she netting two cat on her Sikh lover site

she book them for the meat at the cheese ov her price

The cat and mouse (the computer mouse) imagery and the cheese suggest she catches men who are motivated by sexual attraction (meat). Far from being jealous, Singh seems proud of his new bride's ability to do this. There has even been a suggestion that she is running a dating agency for Sikhs. Cheese and meat are also used because they may well be products sold in Singh's shop.

Singh's wife seems to show no respect to his parents:

she effing at my mum

in all di colours of Punjabi

den stumble like a drunk

malking fun at my daddy.

In the next stanza she is described in contrasting similes that suggest both danger on the one hand and cuteness on the other: his wife has

tiny eyes of a gun

and the tummy of a teddy

His wife deliberately rebels against the expectations of Singh's parents. She has a 'red crew cut' and the clothes she wears (a Tartan sari) suggest she has absorbed some parts of Western culture, while rejecting the work ethic of her husband's parents' generation. Her hair style and her tartan sari can be seen as signs of assimilation, but are also visually funny; as is the donkey jacket she wears. She mimics his father too – showing a lack of respect. We can imagine that Singh's father runs a very efficient shop which is clean and where the bread is not stale and the milk is not out of date.

The customers' voices are heard again complaining about the products in the shop – Singh has neglected all this because he would rather be upstairs making love to his wife. The customers complain that Singh's shop is

…di worst Indian shop

In de whole Indian road

I do not think this is intended to be racist. It is race-related, because of the stereotype of Indians running corner shops, but in the poem Singh would be the first to admit that he does not care about the shop – he shuts it in order to make love to his new bride, when the whole idea of such a shop is that it is open all hours. In fact, Singh's laziness over the shop and his enthusiasm for his new bride both undercut the stereotype of the Indian corner shop owner who is only and exclusively concerned with business.

Line 43 begins a lovely romantic interlude. At midnight, Singh says, he and his wife 'cum down whispering stairs' to sit together on the stool behind the counter and stare out of the shop's windows. The shop is part of a precinct which is 'concrete cold' at night and suggests an uninspiring urban location. Beyond the shop window, beyond the community which criticizes Singh's abilities as a shopkeeper and they see

all di beaches ov di UK in de brightey moon.

They stare past

… di half-price window signs

which suggests they do not care about them.

We then hear his wife speak for the first time in the poem. She asks him

How much do yoo charge for dat moon baby?

He tells her it is half the price of her and that in itself is priceless, so she must be doubly priceless. And so the poem ends on a note of intense romantic tenderness.

His wife's question is deliberately couched in financial terms: corner shops might have all sorts of offers – things that are half-price or on special offer or three for the price of two, but true love and passion cannot be bought and sold and has no price.

Singh does not care about running his shop efficiently; he only cares about his wife and her pleasure. This is a love poem and a poem about rebelling against the expectations of your parents and the community.

Why?

This hilarious poem is full of tender, romantic love

- explores the cultural fusion of second generation British Indians;

- rejects the work ethic and materialism of older generations;

- shows a character rejecting the role picked out for him by his father;

- imitates accent and uses non-Standard English to give us an authentic sense of character and culture;

- subverts traditional stereotypes of British-Asian behaviour;

- is comic and exuberant, while also giving a sense that the couple feel trapped by the shop they run;

- presents a couple engaged in a fulfilling and loving relationship.

'Climbing My Grandfather' – Andrew Waterhouse

Context

Andrew Waterhouse (27 November 1958 Lincolnshire - 20 October 2001) was a British poet, and musician. He grew up in Scarborough and moved to Gainsborough where his parents ran the local Conservative Club, the river allotments and paved streets which feature in his early poetry are all still where he would have remembered them, and he was educated at Gainsborough Grammar School. He studied at Newcastle University, and Wye College, taking an MSc. in environmental science. He lectured at Kirkley Hall Agricultural College. Drawing on his background in this semi-industrial town his early poetry reflects on the town and his family and is evocative of the period (1970s) and the place. He wrote for green journals, and took part in the Trees for Life programme for world reforestation. In 2001 he took his own life.

brogues – a stout, solid shoe.

traverse – a passage across the face of a rock in mountaineering.

good purchase – a good, solid grip.

screed – a smooth area.

Who? Waterhouse imagines himself as very, very tiny and, in a witty extended metaphor, imagines his grandfather as a mountain which he climbs.

When? No specific time.

Where? No specific place.

What? Climbing carefully – with several words from mountaineering – Waterhouse finally reaches the summit – his grandfather's head!

Commentary

Andrew Waterhouse's 'Climbing My Grandfather' is a delightful poem, full of love and nostalgia based around a single extended metaphor or conceit: that the grandfather is a mountain and that the poet or speaker is a mountaineer. The main focus is the grandfather, but the poem makes use of several words from the world of mountaineering or climbing to keep the metaphor going. The extended metaphor is a witty conceit and Waterhouse (although he uses the present tense to give a sense of immediacy) must be writing about a time when he was very small and his grandfather was relatively huge in his young eyes. Of course, for the extended metaphor to make complete sense we must imagine that Waterhouse is very, very tiny in comparison with the mountain that is his grandfather.

The poem opens with a statement of intent in the present tense which at once brings a sense of immediacy to the poem:

I decide to do it free, without a rope or net.

Free climbing is a form of rock climbing specifically contrasted with aid climbing. Like aid climbing, it may use ropes and other means of climbing protection, but only to protect against injury during falls, and not to assist progress. Ropes can be used in free climbing but not to aid upward progress – which must be achieved solely by the mountaineer's hands.

He first makes his way onto his grandfather's sturdy shoes – his brogues and from there 'scramble[s] onto his trousers'. He is scrambling, of course, because he is free climbing. He pushes into his trousers, 'trying to get a grip', a handhold. His grandfather is presented with some vocabulary that would also suit a mountain – 'his <u>overhanging</u> shirt' – like an overhanging crag.

Then in another word specific to mountaineering he 'traverse[s] along his belt/to an earth-stained hand; suggesting that his grandfather is a keen gardener. He tells us that the nails are splintered and give 'good purchase' – and 'good purchase' is essential if you are free climbing. In an oxymoronic simile we are told his grandfather's skin on his fingers is like 'warm ice': his living fingers are alive and warm, but ice continues the mountaineering metaphor, since the higher you climb the more likely you are to encounter ice and snow.

Waterhouse discovers the 'glassy ridge of a scar' on his grandfather's arm, but 'place my feet gently in the old stitches and move on.' He rests for a while 'at his firm shoulder', but I very careful not to look down because 'climbing has its dangers'. He then pulls himself up by the loose skin of his grandfather's neck and stops at his mouth – 'to drink among teeth' – a metaphor which suggests he gives his grandfather a kiss.

'Refreshed' he continues upwards across the 'screed cheek'. He stares into his grandfather's brown eyes, before going up over the forehead and finding the wrinkles there offer numerous handholds and are 'well-spaced and easy.' He reaches his grandfather's 'thick hair (soft and white at this altitude)' and finally reaches the summit. The white hair clearly represents the snow that is found at the top of high mountains. Exhausted and elated by his climb, 'gasping for breath', he lies down in contentment:

Watching clouds and birds circle,

Feeling his heat, knowing

The slow pulse of his good heart.

'Climbing My Grandfather' is written as one extended stanza with regular line lengths but does not use rhyme. It is given coherence by the extended metaphor and Waterhouse's consistent use of words from mountains and from climbing.

The speaker's act is brave: he chooses to climb free and keeps on going at high altitudes, even when he encounters metaphorical ice and snow. We don't learn much about the grandfather but his tolerance is implied:

in the extended metaphor he allows his grandson to climb him. And, equally, the grandson shows respect for his grandfather – he places his feet 'gently in the old stitches of the scar on his arm. He also shows affection by kissing him.

'Climbing My Grandfather' is based on a witty extended metaphor which is inherently amusing, but it is much more than that. In one sense it can be seen as a tribute to mountaineering – especially free climbing – and the vocabulary that Waterhouse uses demonstrates that. Much more importantly, it is a tribute to the poet's grandfather and the love the poet has for him and for his 'good heart'.

Andrew Waterhouse's 'Climbing My Grandfather':

- uses a witty extended metaphor to explore his relationship with his grandfather;

- is a tribute to the love he felt for his grandfather and his grandfather's 'good heart';

- also displays a passion for climbing and mountaineering;

- exudes a tone of genial good humour;

- presents love in a family across the generations;

- overall has a tone of light-hearted playfulness which comes from the slightly surreal nature of the poem's extended metaphor.

Glossary

The Oxford Concise Dictionary of Literary Terms has been invaluable in writing this section of the book. I would again remind the reader that knowledge of these terms is only the start – do NOT define a word you find here in the examination. You can take it for granted that the examiner knows the term: it is up to you to try to use it confidently and with precision and to explain why the poet uses it or what effect it has on the reader.

ALLITERATION the repetition of the same sounds – usually initial consonants or stressed syllables – in any sequence of closely adjacent words.

ALLUSION an indirect or passing reference to some event, person, place or artistic work which is not explained by the writer, but which relies on the reader's familiarity with it.

AMBIGUITY openness to different interpretations.

ANAPHORA

ASSONANCE the repetition of similar vowel sounds in neighbouring words.

BALLAD a folk song or orally transmitted poem telling in a simple and direct way a story with a tragic ending. Ballads are normally composed in quatrains with the second and fourth lines rhyming. Such quatrains are known as the ballad stanza because of its frequent use in what we call ballads.

BLANK VERSE unrhymed lines of ten syllable length. This is a widely used form by Shakespeare in his plays, by Milton and by Wordsworth.

CAESURA	any pause in a line of verse caused by punctuation. This can draw attention to what precedes or follows the caesura and also, by breaking up the rhythm of the line, can slow the poem down and make it more like ordinary speech.
CANON	a body of writings recognized by authority. The canon of a national literature is a body of writings especially approved by critics or anthologists and deemed suitable for academic study. Towards the end of the 20th century there was a general feeling that the canon of English Literature was dominated by dead white men and since then there has been a deliberate and fruitful attempt made to give more prominence to writing by women and by writers from non-white backgrounds. Even your Anthology is a contribution to the canon, because someone sat down and decided that the poems included in it were worthy of study by students taking GCSE.
CARPE DIEM	a Latin phrase from the Roman poet Horace which means 'seize the day' – 'make the best of the present moment'. It is a very common theme of European lyric poetry, in which the speaker of a poem argues that since time is short and death is inevitable, pleasure should be enjoyed while there is still time.
COLLOCATION	the act of putting two words together. What this means in practice is that certain words have very common collocations – in other words they are usually found in written or spoken English in collocation with other words. For example, the

word *Christmas* is often collocated with words such as *cards, presents, carols, holidays,* but you won't often find it collocated with *sadness.* This can be an important term because poets, who are seeking to use words in original ways, will often put two words together are not often collocated.

COLLOQUIALISM the use of informal expressions or vocabulary appropriate to everyday speech rather than the formality of writing. When used in poetry it can make the poem seem more down-to-earth and real, more honest and intimate.

CONCEIT an unusually far-fetched metaphor presenting a surprising and witty parallel between two apparently dissimilar things or feelings.

CONSONANCE the repetition of identical or similar consonants in neighbouring words whose vowel sounds are different.

CONTEXT the biographical, social, cultural and historical circumstances in which a text is produced and read and understood – you might to think of it as its background. However, it is important sometimes to consider the reader's own context – especially when we look back at poems from the Literary Heritage. To interpret a poem with full regard to its background is to contextualize it.

COUPLET a pair of rhyming verse lines, usually of the same length.

CROSSED RHYME the rhyming of one word in the middle of a long line of poetry with a word in a similar position in the next line.

DIALECT — a distinctive variety of language, spoken by members of an identifiable regional group, nation or social class. Dialects differ from one another in pronunciation, vocabulary and grammar. Traditionally they have been looked down on and viewed as variations from an educated 'standard' form of the language, but linguists point out that standard forms themselves are merely dialects which have come to dominate for social and political reasons. In English this notion of dialect is especially important because English is spoken all over the world and there are variations between the English spoken in, say, Yorkshire, Delhi and Australia. Dialects now are increasingly celebrated as a distinct way of speaking and writing which are integral to our identity.

DICTION — the choice of words used in any literary work.

DISSONANCE — harshness of sound.

DRAMATIC MONOLOGUE — a kind of poem in which a single fictional or historical character (not the poet) speaks to a silent audience and unwittingly reveals the truth about their character.

ELEGY — a lyric poem lamenting the death of a friend or public figure or reflecting seriously on a serious subject. The elegiac has come to refer to the mournful mood of such poems.

ELLIPSIS	the omission from a sentence of a word or words which would be required for complete clarity. It is used all the time in everyday speech, but is often used in poetry to promote compression and/or ambiguity. The adjective is elliptical.
END-RHYME	rhyme occurring at the end of a line of poetry. The most common form of rhyme.
END-STOPPED	a line of poetry brought to a pause by the use of punctuation. The opposite of enjambment.
ENJAMBMENT	caused by the lack of punctuation at the end of a line of poetry, this causes the sense (and the voice when the poem is read aloud) to 'run over' into the next line. In general, this can impart to poems the feel of ordinary speech, but there are examples in the Anthology of more precise reasons for the poet to use enjambment.
EPIPHANY	a sudden moment of insight or revelation, usually at the end of a poem.
EPIZEUXIS	the technique by which a word is repeated for emphasis with no other words intervening
EUPHONY	a pleasing smoothness of sound
FALLING RHYTHM	the effect produced by several lines in succession which end with a feminine ending
FEMININE ENDING	the ending of a line of poetry on an unstressed syllable
FIGURATIVE	Not literal. Obviously 'figurative' language covers metaphor and simile and personification
FIGURE OF SPEECH	any expression which departs from the

ordinary literal sense or normal order of words. Figurative language (the opposite of literal language) includes metaphor, simile and personification. Some figures of speech – such as alliteration and assonance achieve their effects through the repetition of sounds.

FOREGROUNDING

giving unusual prominence to one part of a text. Poetry differs from everyday speech and prose by its use of regular rhythm, metaphors, alliteration and other devices by which its language draws attention to itself.

FREE VERSE

a kind of poetry that does not conform to any regular pattern of line length or rhyme. The length of its lines are irregular as its use of rhyme – if any.

HALF-RHYME

an imperfect rhyme – also known as para-rhyme, near rhyme and slant rhyme – in which the final consonants but the vowel sounds do not match. Pioneered in the 19th century by the Emily Dickinson and Gerard Manley Hopkins, and made even more popular by Wilfred Owen and T S Eliot in the early 20th century,

HOMONYM

a word that is identical to another word either in sound or in spelling

HOMOPHONE

a word that is pronounced in the same way as another word but which differs in meaning and/or spelling.

HYPERBOLE	exaggeration for the sake of emphasis.
IDIOM	an everyday phrase that cannot be translated literally because its meaning does not correspond to the specific words in the phrase. There are thousands in English like – *you get up my nose, when pigs fly, she was all ears*.
IMAGERY	a rather vague critical term covering literal and metaphorical language which evoke sense impressions with reference to concrete objects – the things the writer describes.
INTERNAL RHYME	a poetic device in which two or more words in the same line rhyme.
INTERTEXTUALITY	the relationship that a text may have with anoth preceding and usually well-known text.
INVERSION	the reversal of the normally expected order or words. 'Normally expected' means how we might say the words in the order of normal speech; to invert the normal word order usually draws attention or foregrounds the words.
JUXTAPOSITION	two things that are placed alongside each other.
LAMENT	any poem expressing profound grief usually in the face of death.
LATINATE	Latinate diction in English means the use of words derived from Latin rather than those derived from Old English.
LITOTES	understatement – the opposite of hyperbole.
LYRIC	any fairly short poem expressing the personal

mood of the speaker.

METAPHOR
the most important figure of speech in which in which one thing is referred to by a word normally associated with another thing, so as to suggest some common quality shared by both things. In metaphor, this similarity is directly stated, unlike in a simile where the resemblance is indirect and introduced by the words like or as. Much of our everyday language is made up of metaphor too — to say someone is as greedy as a pig is a simile; to say he is a pig is a metaphor.

MNEMONIC
a form of words or letters that helps people remember things. It is common in everyday sayings and uses some of the features of language that we associate with poetry. For example, the weather saying Red sky at night, shepherd's delight uses rhyme.

MONOLOGUE`
an extended speech uttered by one speaker.

NARRATOR
the one who tells or is assumed to be the voice of the poem.

OCTAVE or OCTET
a group of eight lines forming the first part of a sonnet.

ONOMATOPOEIA
the use of words that seem to imitate the sounds they refer to (*bang, whizz, crackle, fizz*) or any combination or words in which the sound echoes or seems to echo the sense. The adjective is onomatopoeic, so you can say that *blast* is an onomatopoeic word.

ORAL TRADITION
the passing on from one generation to another of songs, chants, poems, proverbs by word of

mouth and memory.

OXYMORON a figure of speech that combines two seemingly contradictory terms as in the everyday terms bitter-sweet and living death.

PARALLELISM the arrangement of similarly constructed clause, sentences or lines of poetry.

PARADOX a statement which is self-contradictory.

PATHETIC FALLACY this is the convention that natural phenomena (usually the weather) are a reflection of the poet's or the narrator's mood. It may well involve the personification of things in nature, but does not have to. At its simplest, a writer might choose to associate very bad weather with a mood of depression and sadness.

PERSONA the assumed identity or fictional narrator assumed by a writer.

PERSONIFICATION a figure of speech in which animals, abstract ideas or lifeless things are referred to as if they were human. Sometimes known as personal metaphor.

PETRARCHAN characteristic of the Italian poet Petrarch (1304 – 1374). Mainly applied to the Petrarchan sonnet which is different in its form from the Shakespearean sonnet.

PHONETIC SPELLING a technique writers use which involves misspelling a word in order to imitate the accent in which the word is said.

PLOSIVE

explosive. Used to describe sounds that we form by putting our lips together such as *b* and *p*.

POSTCOLONIAL LITERATURE

a term devised to describe what used to be called Commonwealth Literature (and before that Empire Writing!). The term covers a very wide range of writing from countries that were once colonies of European countries. It has come to include some writing by writers of non-white racial backgrounds whose roots or family originated in former colonies – no matter where they live now.

PUN

an expression that derives humour either through using a word that has two distinct meanings or two similar sounding words (homophones).

QUATRAIN

a verse stanza of four lines – usually rhymed.

REFRAIN

a line, or a group of lines, repeated at intervals throughout a poem – usually at regular intervals and at the end of a stanza.

RHYME

the identity of sound between syllables or paired groups of syllables usually at the end of a line of poetry.

RHYME SCHEME

the pattern in which the rhymed line endings are arranged in any poem or stanza. This is normally written as a sequence of letters where each line ending in the same rhyme is given the same alphabetical letter. So a Shakespearean sonnet's rhyme scheme is ababcdcdefefgg, but the rhyme scheme of a Petrarchan sonnet is abbaabbacdecde. In other poems the rhyme scheme might be arranged to suit the poet's convenience or intentions. For example, in Blake's 'London' the first stanza rhymes abab, the second cdcd and so on.

RHYTHM
a pattern of sounds which is repeated with the stress falling on the same syllables (more or less) in each line. However, variations to the pattern, especially towards the end of the poem, often stand out and are foregrounded because they break the pattern the poet has built up through the course of the poem.

ROMANTICISM
the name given to the artistic movement that emerged in England and Germany in the 19790a and in the rest of Europe in the 1820s and beyond. It was a movement that saw great changes in literature, painting, sculpture, architecture and music and found its catalyst in the new philosophical ideas of Jean Jacques Rousseau and Thomas Paine, and in response to the French and industrial revolutions. Its chief emphasis was on freedom of individual self-expression, sincerity, spontaneity and originality, but it also looked to the distant past of the Middle Ages for some of its inspiration.

SATIRE
any type of writing which exposes and mocks the foolishness or evil of individuals, institutions or societies. A poem can be satiric (adjective) or you

can say a poet satirizes something or somebody.

SESTET   a group of six lines forming the second half of a sonnet, following the octet.

SIBILANCE   the noticeable recurrence of *s* sounds.

SIMILE   an explicit comparison between two different things, actions or feelings, usually introduced by *like* or *as*.

SONNET   a lyric poem of 14 lines of equal length. The form originated in Italy and was made famous as a vehicle for love poetry by Petrarch and came to be adopted throughout Europe. The standard subject matter of early sonnets was romantic love, but in the 17th century John Donne used it to write religious poetry and John Milton wrote political sonnets, so it came to be used for any subject matter. The sonnet form enjoyed a revival in the Romantic period (Wordsworth, Keats and Shelley all wrote them) and continues to be widely used today. Some poets have written connected series of sonnets and these are known as sonnet cycles. Petrarchan sonnets differ slightly in their rhyme scheme from Shakespearean sonnets (see the entry above on rhyme scheme). A Petrarchan sonnet consists of two quatrains (the octet) followed by two tercets (the sestet). A Shakespearean sonnet consist of two quatrains (the octet) followed by another quatrain and a final couplet (the sestet).

STANZA   a group of verse lines forming a section of a poem and sharing the same structure in terms of the length of the lines, the rhyme scheme and the rhythm.

STYLE	any specific way of using language, which is characteristic of an author, a period, a type of poetry or a group of writers.
SYLLOGISM	a form of logical argument that draws a conclusion from two propositions. It is very characteristic of Metaphysical poetry and is exemplified in the anthology by Marvell's 'To His Coy Mistress'.
SYMBOL	anything that represents something else. A national flag symbolizes the country that uses it; symbols are heavily used in road signs. In poetry symbols can represent almost anything. Blake's 'The Sick Rose' and Armitage's 'Harmonium' are two good examples of symbols dealt with in this book.
SYNECDOCHE	a figure of speech in which a thing or person is referred to indirectly, either by naming some part of it (*hands* for manual labourers) or by naming some big thing of which it is a part (the law for police officers). As you can see from these examples, it is a common practice in speech.
TONE	a critical term meaning the mood or atmosphere of a piece of writing. It may also include the sense of the writer's attitude to the reader of the subject matter.
TURN	the English term for a sudden change in mood or line of argument, especially in line 9 of a sonnet.
VERSE	another word for poetry as opposed to prose. The use of the word 'verse' sometimes implies writing that rhymes and has a rhythm, but perhaps lacks the merit of real poetry.
VERISIMILITUDE	truth-like; giving a strong sense of reality.

VERSE PARAGRAPH	a group of lines of poetry forming a section of a poem, the length of the unit being determined by the sense rather than a particular stanza pattern.
VOLTA	the Italian term for the 'turn' in the argument or mood of a sonnet which normally occurs in the ninth line at the start of the sestet, but sometimes in Shakespearean sonnets is delayed until the final couplet.
WIT	a general term which covers the idea of intelligence, but refers in poetry more specifically to verbal ingenuity and cleverness.

CPSIA information can be obtained
at www.ICGtesting.com
Printed in the USA
LVOW13s1442260417

532273LV00009B/935/P